Tribunal

AUTHENTIC INTERPRETATIONS

ON THE 1983 CODE

Lawrence G. Wrenn

D1528505

Canon Law Society of America
Washington, DC 20064

TABLE OF CONTENTS

AUTHENTIC INTERPRETATIONS
ON THE 1983 CODE*

A. SOME PRELIMINARY NOTIONS

1. The Pontifical Commission for the Authentic Interpretation of the Code of Canon Law (the "Code Commission") was established by Pope John Paul II on January 2, 1984 and given the exclusive right to render authentic interpretation of the canons of the *Code of Canon Law* and of other universal laws of the Latin Church.[1] On June 28, 1988, Pope John Paul II, by the Apostolic Constitution *Pastor bonus*, which took effect on March 1, 1989, renamed the commission the Pontifical Council for the Interpretation of Legislative Texts (the "Law Council") and he broadened its competence to include the authentic interpretation of all the universal laws of the Church, including, as later became clear, the then soon to be promulgated *Code of Canons of the Eastern Churches*.[2]

2. The interpretation of law may be defined as *a declaration or an explanation of the true sense already contained, at least obscurely, in a law*.

3. A couple of points may be made regarding this definition. Perhaps the more obvious of the two is that an interpretation is not a reworking or manipulation or distortion of a law in order to impose upon the law a meaning that is really alien to it.

Rather it has always been understood that once a law has been drafted and promulgated (often after years of painstaking research, dialogue and consultation), it then enjoys an intrinsic meaning, intended by the legislator and expressed in certain words. Every canon of the Code, therefore, enjoys an innate, true sense. The work of interpretation is not to change that true sense into something else; rather it is to clarify and to draw out that true meaning when, for one reason or another, it is not perfectly clear.

Having said that, however, the fact is that canonists, even expert canonists, "approved authors" and esteemed professors of pontifical faculties of canon

---

*Presentation given in part to the Canon Law Society of Great Britain and Ireland on May 11, 1993, London Colney, St. Albans, Hertfordshire.

[1]*Communicationes* XVI (1984) 1, 3-4.

[2]*Communicationes* XX (1988) 1, 3, 52-53, 61 and XXIII (1991) 130. For more on the competence of the Law Council see Francisco Javier Urrutia, "De Pontificio Consilio de legum textibus interpretandis," *Periodica* 78 (1989) 503-521.

law around the world, are interpreting law all the time, and oftentimes those "interpretations" are not, in fact, in accord with what has later been declared to be the true sense of the law. Canon 1099, §2 of the 1917 Code, for example, said that children who were "born of non-Catholics" (*ab acatholicis nati*) and who were raised from infancy in heresy, were not bound to the form of marriage. In a commentary published in 1919, the great Swiss-American canonist, Charles Augustine, O.S.B. "interpreted" that phrase "born of non-Catholics" to mean *two* non-Catholics; the term, as found in the canon, was, after all, in the plural.[3] Nevertheless, some ten years later the Code Commission ruled that the phrase "born of non-Catholics" includes those born of parents only *one* of whom is non-Catholic.[4] This was an authentic interpretation by the Code Commission which declared the true sense contained in the law. In retrospect, therefore, it must be concluded that Augustine's contrary opinion did not capture the true sense of the law and that, by definition therefore, it was not an interpretation in the *proper* sense of that word. Augustine's opinion, in other words, was just that: it was an opinion. Or, if you wish (and there is, I think, merit in so wishing) it was an interpretation in the *improper* sense of the term. It was an "interpretation" that did not catch the true sense of the canon.

4.   The second point to be made regarding the definition of interpretation is this: when the definition says that an interpretation can be either a declaration or an explanation, it is talking about two different types of interpretation.

The first type is called a *declarative* interpretation. A declarative interpretation is made when the meaning of the law is not really doubtful in the first place, at least not objectively doubtful. Individual canonists may have some subjective doubt about the meaning, perhaps because they have not thought it through sufficiently,[5] or paid enough attention to the usual methods of resolving doubt, such as text, context, parallel passages, the purpose and circumstances of the law and the mind of the legislator, all of which are mentioned in canon 17. But what is involved here is a law that is not *objectively* doubtful. The meaning indeed is intrinsically certain, *in se certa* as canon 16 says. The purpose of a declarative interpretation, therefore, is simply to make clear or clearer what is already certain. The declarative

---

[3]Charles Augustine, *A Commentary on the New Code of Canon Law* (St. Louis: B. Herder, 1919) V, 302.

[4]*AAS* 21 (1929) 573; *Canon Law Digest* (hereafter *CLD*) 1, 543.

[5]Ludovicus Bender, *Legum Ecclesiasticarum Interpretatio et Suppletio* (Roma: Desclée, 1961) 116 and 305.

interpretation is then the simplest, the most elementary kind of interpretation. Indeed, at a point in history, it was called simply a "declaration," to distinguish it from a genuine interpretation, though even before the 1917 Code, it had come to be accepted as a genuine interpretation but in the broad sense of that term.[6] Examples of each type of interpretation will be offered presently, and though it will be clear from those examples that a declarative interpretation is not always as simple as it might seem, nevertheless the principle remains operative: a declarative interpretation is a statement that clarifies a law about which there was never any objective doubt. Once an authentic declarative interpretation is made, therefore, it has retroactive force, since it merely restates a meaning that was always intrinsically certain.[7]

The second type of interpretation, an interpretation in the strict sense of the term, is called an *explanatory* interpretation. An explanatory interpretation explains a law, the true meaning of which is objectively doubtful; and since a doubtful law is not binding,[8] the law in question would have no binding force until an authentic interpretation resolved the objective doubt. Unlike the declarative interpretation, therefore, an explanatory interpretation does not have retroactive force.[9]

5. The special mandate of the Code Commission/Law Council is to interpret. This refers both to interpretation in the ordinary or *strict* sense of that word (namely an explanatory interpretation), and to interpretation in the *broad* sense (that is, a declarative interpretation). In principle, however, it would not extend to interpretation in the *improper* sense of the word. It is not, in other words, within the ordinary competence of the Commission/Council to issue an "interpretation" that does not reflect the true sense contained in the law. Nevertheless, "to err is human," as Alexander Pope said, and it is not, therefore, inconceivable that the Commission/Council might, on occasion, issue such an interpretation.

When the Commission/Council issues a response, whether it be explanatory or merely declarative (or even, indeed, were it an improper interpretation) it frequently, though not always, either restricts or extends the number of cases

---

[6]Francisco Wernz, *Ius Decretalium* (Romae: Propaganda Fide, 1908) I, 132, para. 127. For an older usage of the word "declaration," see John Rogg Schmidt, *The Principles of Authentic Interpretation in Canon 17 of the Code of Canon Law* (Washington: CUA Press, 1941) 169-177.

[7]Canon 16, §2.

[8]Canon 14.

[9]Canon 16, §2.

3

that would seem warranted by a literal reading of the canon.[10] This might suggest that besides the two types of interpretation already mentioned (declarative and explanatory) there are two other types as well (restrictive and extensive). Indeed most commentators on both the 1917 and the 1983 Codes have taken precisely that position and the wording of the pertinent canon (c. 17, §2 in the 1917 Code and c. 16, §2 in the 1983 Code) seems to corroborate their view.[11] My own sense, however, is that, just as there are basically only two kinds of law (the objectively certain and the objectively doubtful), so there are basically only two kinds of interpretation (declarative and explanatory). Extensive and restrictive interpretation are not, therefore, types but *sub*types of interpretation.

This matter of types and subtypes requires further explanation. The first type of interpretation is a *declarative* interpretation. A declarative interpretation can extend or restrict the obvious meaning of a canon, but when it does so, it should be called not an extensive or restrictive interpretation, but rather a quasi-extensive or quasi-restrictive interpretation, since in a declarative interpretation there is no *real* extension or restriction but only an apparent one, because the practical limits of the law were, in fact, objectively certain all along (and thus, a declarative interpretation that is quasi-extensive or quasi-restrictive is retroactive). The second type of interpretation is an *explanatory* interpretation, and this too can extend or restrict the obvious meaning of a canon, but in this case it is genuinely extensive or restrictive since it is solving an objective doubt in one direction or the other (so the interpretation, as c. 16, §2 indicates, is not retroactive). And finally it should be noted that an *improper* interpretation can likewise extend or restrict, but again should not be called simply extensive or restrictive but rather ultra-extensive or ultra-restrictive since an improper interpretation (which might also be called an ultra-explanatory interpretation) goes beyond the true sense of the law.

---

[10]For example, the 1929 response mentioned above, where the Code Commission ruled that the phrase "born of non-Catholics" included those born of parents only one of whom was non-Catholic, seemed to extend the number of cases beyond those indicated by a literal reading of the canon. After the ruling, in other words, it was clear that more people would be excused from the form of marriage than might previously have been thought.

[11]The present canon 16, §2, for example, reads "An authentic interpretation communicated in the form of law has the same force as the law itself and must be promulgated. Furthermore, if such an interpretation merely declares what was certain in the words of the law in themselves, it has retroactive force; if it restricts or extends the law or if it explains a doubtful law, it is not retroactive."

4

6. Schematically, the various types and subtypes of interpretation may be diagrammed as follows:

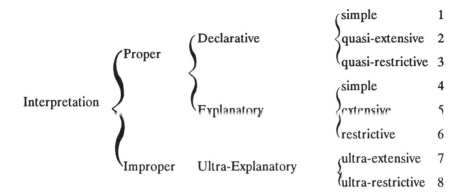

		simple	1
	Declarative	quasi-extensive	2
Proper		quasi-restrictive	3
		simple	4
Interpretation	Explanatory	extensive	5
		restrictive	6
Improper	Ultra-Explanatory	ultra-extensive	7
		ultra-restrictive	8

B. EXAMPLES

According to this schema there are eight subtypes of interpretation. Which seems a lot. So many, indeed, that one wonders whether the entire matter is not being artificially bloated. What would the man of Surrey, William of Occam, think of all this? There was, after all, much wisdom in his famous dictum: *Entia non sunt multiplicanda sine necessitate.* Is that what is happening here? Are categories being needlessly multiplied? I think not. In fact, the following examples, all taken from the 1917 Code, will demonstrate that *fewer* categories would not handle the traffic; they would not adequately describe the full range of responses that have been given and are still being given by the Code Commission.

1. *Simple Declarative.* Canon 1254, §2 said that "all those" (*omnes*) between the ages of twenty-one and fifty-nine were bound to fast. Shortly after the Code was promulgated, the Commission was asked the following, seemingly preposterous question "Whether the word *omnes* . . . applies in the same way to women as to men." On January 13, 1918 the President of the Commission replied "In the affirmative."[12] This clearly is a simple, declarative interpretation.

2. *Quasi-extensive.* It has already been noted (under A 3) that in 1929 the Commission interpreted the phrase "born of non-Catholics" in canon 1099, §2 to include those who born of parents only *one* of whom was non-Catholic. Given the fact that most of the commentators on the 1917 Code had, prior to the 1929 response, held the opposite opinion,[13] it would appear that the canon contained an objective doubt, and that the 1929 response was therefore an explanatory interpretation, or more specifically an extensive interpretation (since it extended the number of people who would be excused from the form of marriage). Several years later, however, the Commission was asked "Whether the interpretation of canon 1099, §2, given on July 20, 1929 is declarative or extensive?". The Commission responded on July 25, 1931 "In the affirmative to the first part; in the negative to the second."[14]

Already, therefore, it is clear that not everything is clear, neither the interpretation itself nor how that interpretation is to be classified. Sometimes

---

[12]*CLD* 1, 593.

[13]Charles Augustine was, in fact, only one of many. See Petrus Card. Gasparri, *Tractatus Canonicus de Matrimonio* (Città del Vaticano: Typis Polyglottis Vaticanis, 1932) II, 145, n. 1025.

[14]*AAS* 23 (1931) 388; *CLD* 1: 544.

what seems to be the obvious interpretation is not the correct one, and what seems to constitute objective doubt is really only subjective. Two observations, however, may be made in defense of the Commission's responses. First, the reasoning behind the 1929 decision, according to Cardinal Gasparri, was that those born of parents only *one* of whom is non-Catholic are, *if they were raised in heresy from infancy,* in the same basic position in terms of marriage as those born of *two* non-Catholic parents. Thus there is no apparent reason why those who have one non-Catholic parent would be *held* to the form of marriage while those who had two non-Catholic parents would be *excused* from it.[15] Secondly, as early as 1919, the Commission had already declared that the phrase "children of non-Catholics" (*filii acatholicorum*) in canon 987 (regarding those impeded from ordination) should be interpreted to include those born of parents only one of whom was non-Catholic.[16]

Despite, therefore, the many outstanding canonists who were undoubtedly taken aback at the time, both the 1929 response of the Commission and the later response stating that the 1929 interpretation was only declarative and not extensive, were, nevertheless broadly and firmly grounded.

While it is true, however, that the 1929 response was not extensive, it is nevertheless accurate, (and this really is the whole point here) to describe it as quasi-extensive, since the interpretation *seems* or *appears* to extend the number of people who are excused from the form of marriage beyond those indicated by a strict reading of the letter of the law.

3.   *Quasi-restrictive.* Canon 542 had said that "those who had adhered to a non-Catholic sect" (*qui sectae acatholicae adhaeserunt*) would not be validly admitted into a novitiate. On October 16, 1919 the Commission said that, in effect, this phrase should not be read too literally. The canon did not really mean everybody who had adhered to a non-Catholic sect but only those who had once been Catholic but then "fell away" (*defecerunt*) and adhered to a non-Catholic sect.[17]

Clearly this is at least quasi-restrictive. The question is, was it more than that? Was it truly restrictive? Or to put the question in another way, was the doubt that prompted the question just subjective so that the response was merely declarative, or was it an objective doubt, making the response

[15]Gasparri, op. cit., II, 146, n. 1027.
[16]*AAS* 11 (1919) 478; *CLD* 1: 487.
[17]*AAS* 11 (1919) 477; *CLD* 1: 298.

7

explanatory? The answer, it seems, is that there was no really objective doubt here since it can be assumed that a reasonable legislator would certainly not have wanted to penalize a person who grew up as a non-Catholic (and therefore "had adhered to a non-Catholic sect") but then became a Catholic and wanted to enter a religious community. All along, in other words, the *true* sense of the law referred only to those who were raised as Catholics, then "fell away" and finally returned. Vermeersch-Creusen aptly referred to the Commission's response as a "declaration."[18]

4. *Simple Explanatory.* Canon 1098 had said that a couple could contract marriage before two witnesses only, and without the presence of a priest, if a competent priest "could neither be had nor reached without grave inconvenience" (*si haberi vel adiri nequeat sine gravi incommodo*). Did this mean that the couple could marry validly before two witnesses only if the priest was *physically* absent, or could they do so even if the priest was just *morally* absent, i.e., unable to perform the ceremony for some reason? On March 10, 1928 the Commission issued the following question and answer: Whether canon 1098 is to be understood as referring only to the physical absence of the pastor or Ordinary of the place? Reply: In the affirmative.[19]

At first blush the Commission's response seems fairly straightforward and does not seem to involve the solution of an objective doubt, so classifying the response as explanatory seems questionable at best. Nevertheless the fact is that a few years later the Commission issued a second response on the same question (a response which will be examined presently since it serves as the example for the next category, i.e., extensive interpretation). This second response was so at odds with the first response that it seems proper to conclude, given the fact that the Commission itself apparently could not make up its mind on the subject, that there must have been an objective doubt present.

5. *Extensive.* On July 25, 1931 the Commission issued the following question and answer: Whether the "physical absence of the pastor or Ordinary," mentioned in the reply of March 10, 1928, includes also a case where the pastor or Ordinary, although materially present in the place, is unable by reason of grave inconvenience to assist at the marriage asking and receiving

---

[18]A. Vermeersch and J. Creusen, *Epitome Iuris Canonici* (Romae: Dessain, 1932) I, 483, n. 673.

[19]*AAS* 20 (1928) 120; *CLD* 1: 542.

the consent of the contracting parties. Reply: In the affirmative.[20]

Given these two responses of 1928 and 1931, and assuming that the first is not dead wrong, the logical conclusions seem to be: 1) that the first response requiring physical absence was a simple explanatory interpretation; and 2) that the second response, extending the meaning of physical absence to include a kind of moral absence, was an extensive interpretation.

It is entirely possible, of course, that the first response, that of 1928, was, in fact, dead wrong, as Amleto Cardinal Cicognani suggested when he said that the second response "apparently revises" the first.[21] But classifying the first response as simple explanatory and the second as extensive would seem, first of all, to reflect more faithfully the actual wording of the two responses, and secondly to be the position, at least by extrapolation, of most of the authors.[22]

6. *Restrictive.* Canon 423 noted that the college of consultors in a diocese is to be composed of "priests" (*sacerdotes*). Beyond noting that a consultor should be endowed with holiness, good morals, sound doctrine and prudence, the Code itself put no further restrictions on those priests who might be eligible for the office of consultor. In 1931, however, the Commission ruled that, in fact, not all priests were eligible, that not only were religious priests excluded but so also were diocesan priests who had formerly been religious.[23] This seems to be a truly restrictive interpretation, explaining a law about which there was some objective doubt.

7. *Ultra-extensive.* Presumably the Commission/Council has never, in fact, given an ultra-extensive interpretation. Cardinal Castillo Lara, indeed, in his 1988 address in Vienna to the Canon Law Society of Austria, specifically noted that the Commission does not indulge in any sort of interpretation which would, in effect, establish a materially new law, and that any "interpretation" of that sort would be beyond the ordinary competence of the Commis-

---

[20]*AAS* 23 (1931) 388; *CLD* 1: 542. For still another response on the same subject, see *AAS* 37 (1945) 149; *CLD* 3: 454.

[21]Amleto Cicognani, *Canon Law*, 2nd rev. ed. (Westminster: Newman Bookshop, 1934) 615.

[22]See, for example, Gasparri, op. cit., II, 142, n. 1017 and Franciscus Wernz and Petrus Vidal, *Ius Canonicum*, V, *Ius Matrimoniale* (Romae: Gregorian University, 1946) 697, n. 73*. The position of Gasparri and Wernz-Vidal seems to differ only marginally from my own. Theirs is that physical absence means physical inability to officiate on account of a grave inconvenience; mine is that physical absence includes moral inability to officiate.

[23]*AAS* 23 (1931) 110; *CLD* 1:241-242.

sion.[24]

Nevertheless an example of an ultra-extensive interpretation might be this: given the Commission's ruling on canon 542, mentioned under B 3, that restricted the application of the phrase "those who had adhered to a non-Catholic sect" to "fallen away" Catholics, the opinion that would extend that phrase to include those who had been born and raised as Protestants would clearly be an ultra-extensive interpretation, since it would extend the meaning of the canon beyond what has been authentically declared to be the true sense of the law.

8. *Ultra-restrictive.* Although Cardinal Cicognani seemed to imply that the Commission did, in fact, issue an ultra-restrictive interpretation when it ruled that canon 1098 allowed a couple to marry before witnesses alone only when the priest was *physically* absent,[25] nevertheless Cardinal Castillo Lara's remarks about any such interpretation being beyond the powers of the Commission certainly apply here. In general, it is assumed that the Commission/Council never issues an "interpretation" that goes beyond the true sense of the law.

As for an example of an ultra-restrictive interpretation, we have already seen one. When Charles Augustine and most of the commentators on canon 1099, §2 interpreted the phrase "born of non-Catholics" to mean *two* non-Catholics, they were, given the authentic and broader interpretation of 1929, engaging in an ultra-restrictive interpretation. Such an interpretation was more restrictive than the true sense of the law as later defined by the Commission.

---

[24]*Communicationes* XX (1988) 281.
[25]See B 4 and footnote 21. See also Cicognani, op. cit., 434.

10

C. CLASSIFYING THE RESPONSES OF THE COMMISSION/COUNCIL ON THE 1983 CODE

Let us examine now the first twenty-four Responses on the 1983 Code (twenty-six actually, since numbers 3 and 8 each contain a double question and answer) and attempt to classify them. They are treated in the order in which they were published in the *Acta Apostolicae Sedis*.

1. Holy Communion Permitted Only Twice on the Same Day

The Doubt: Whether, according to canon 917, one who has already received the Most Holy Eucharist may receive it on the same day only a second time, or as often as one participates in the celebration of the Eucharist.

The Response: Affirmative to the first; negative to the second.[26]

Canon 917 says that "a person who has received the Most Holy Eucharist may receive it again (*iterum*) on the same day only during the celebration of the Eucharist in which the person participates."[27]

The doubt regarding this canon stems from the use of that ambiguous word *iterum* which, as is well known and as Justinian noted long ago in the *Digest*, can mean either "a second time" or "again."[28]

It is clear from the *Communicationes* account that, when this canon was being drafted in 1978, although there was some concern and discussion among the consultors about the possible dangers of excessive liberalization, nevertheless "practically all" the consultors favored the right of a properly disposed person to receive Holy Communion not just a second time but as often as he or she participates in the celebration of Mass.[29] It was with this mindset, that the canon, using the word *iterum*, was drafted.

This opinion of "practically all" the Consultors favoring the broader sense

---

[26]*AAS* 76 (1984) 746; *Periodica* 73 (1984) 285-287.

[27]From the CLSA translation. The translation of the CLSGBI is substantially the same.

[28]D 2, 13, 7.

[29]*Communicationes* XIII (1981) 414-415. The reasoning of the consultors was basically this: in the celebration of the Eucharist, the sacrifice of Christ is re-presented in the memorial supper; full participation, therefore, consists in eating the food of this supper, and to deny that food to a properly disposed person participating in the supper is not in harmony with the spirit of the celebration.

11

of the word *iterum* surely constituted a solidly probable position. When, therefore, the Commission ruled in favor of the narrower sense of the word, it was, it seems, solving an objective doubt.   This interpretation of the Commission was, therefore, a truly RESTRICTIVE interpretation, and so was not retroactive. Prior to the ruling, people were free to receive the Eucharist as often as they participated at Mass; after the ruling they were permitted to receive only twice on the same day.

2. The Nonnecessity of Using the Documentary Process for Simple Lack of Form Cases

The Doubt: Whether, in order to prove the state of freedom of those who, although bound to the canonical form, attempted marriage before a civil official or a non-Catholic minister, the documentary process mentioned in canon 1686 is necessarily required, or the pre-nuptial investigation dealt with in canons 1066-1067 suffices.

The Response: Negative to the first; affirmative to the second.[30]

There are basically two types of lack of form cases: the simple and the more complicated. The simple type is the one in which a Catholic, without obtaining a dispensation from the form, marries before a civil official or non-Catholic minister. The more complicated type occurs when the form is observed to some degree but invalidly, as, for example, when the priest is not properly delegated or when only one witness is present.

Under the old law, i.e., the law prior to *Causas matrimoniales*, Article 231 §1 of the 1936 Instruction *Provida* made it clear that the simple lack of form case could be handled administratively and did not require a judicial process of any kind.[31] The more complicated type, however, required the full judicial process since canon 1990 of the 1917 Code allowed the documentary or informal process only for certain selected impediments.

With the promulgation of *Causas matrimoniales* in 1971, however, the availability of the documentary process was extended, by Norm XI, to include cases based "on defect of canonical form."[32] Given the fact that the express purpose of Pope Paul VI in promulgating those norms was to expedite the matrimonial process,[33] and not to slow it down or make it more cumbersome, it was widely assumed that Norm XI applied only to the more complicated type of lack of form case. If such a case, in other words, met the usual requirements of a documentary procedure, it could, after March 28, 1971, be handled by the informal rather than the formal judicial process. But the sense was, at least in the United States, that the simple type of lack of form case could continue to be handled by a simple administrative procedure.

---

[30]*AAS* 76 (1984) 747; *Periodica* 73 (1984) 287-290.

[31]*AAS* 28 (1936) 359.

[32]*AAS* 63 (1971) 445 — *ex defectu formae canonicae.*

[33]*AAS* 63 (1971) 442 — *expeditior fiat ipse matrimonialis processus.*

13

Some commentators on *Causas matrimoniales*, however, were of the opinion, for reasons that we need not get into here, that Norm XI was saying that the simple type of lack of form case could no longer be handled by an administrative procedure but now required the informal judicial process.[34]

Although the opinion of these commentators was not without merit, the practice of handling simple lack of form cases by an administrative procedure continued, and when the coetus for the revision of procedural law met in 1979 to discuss the documentary process, they changed the phrase "lack of form" to "lack of legitimate form" precisely so that it would be clear that a simple lack of form case did not require any process at all but that a simple administrative procedure sufficed.[35]

It would seem, therefore, that by the time the 1983 Code was promulgated, there was little if any doubt about this matter, certainly no objective doubt. The response of the Code Commission was therefore declarative and not explanatory. But the next question is this: is it a simple declarative response or is it quasi-extensive or quasi-restrictive? It is not quasi-restrictive since the response does not say that the documentary process *may* not be applied to a simple lack of form case but merely that it *need* not be. Nor is it quasi-extensive since the response does not necessarily extend the number of cases beyond those clearly intended by the law. The law, in other words, at least by implication, allows the administrative procedure for the simple lack of form case, which is precisely what the response of the Commission says, no more and no less. The response, therefore, is a SIMPLE DECLARATIVE one.

[34]See, for example, Orlando DiJorio, "Annotationes in M. Causas Matrimoniales," *Periodica* 65 (1976) 359-361.

[35]*Communicationes* XI (1979) 269.

3. The Stability and Replacement of A Consultor

I. The Doubt: Whether, according to canon 502, §1, a member of the college of consultors who ceases to be a member of the presbyteral council remains in office as consultor.

The Response: Affirmative.

II. The Doubt: Whether during the five year term, if a consultor ceases from office, the diocesan bishop must appoint another to replace him.

The Response: Negative and "ad mentem." The mind of the legislator is that an obligation to appoint another consultor exists only when the minimum number required by canon 502, §1 was lacking.[36]

Canon 502, §1 states "some priests are to be freely selected by the diocesan bishop from among the members of the presbyteral council to constitute a college of consultors."

At the October 1981 plenary session of the Commission, two of the Fathers recommended that the words "from among the members of the presbyteral council" be dropped since there was no valid reason for that requirement. The position of the Commission, however, was that the text should remain as is because the college of consultors is seen as a specific group, a "*coetus restrictus*" of the presbyteral council. Having this "*coetus restrictus*" of the council is useful, said the Commission, first, because it would be inconvenient, especially in large dioceses, to conduct frequent meetings of the entire presbyteral council; and secondly, because there are some highly delicate questions that are better discussed with a smaller group.[37]

This characterization of the college as a kind of inner circle of the presbyteral council led to considerable confusion and was no doubt the principal factor that gave rise to the doubt on the part of some about whether a consultor who ceased to be a council member would remain in office as a consultor. Obviously, if the college were really an inner circle of the council, then if one ceased to be a member of the whole council, one would automatically cease to be a member of the inner circle of that council as well.

---

[36]*AAS* 76 (1984) 747; *Periodica* 73 (1984) 290-292.
[37]*Communicationes* XIV (1982) 217-218.

15

In fact, however, it has been generally understood that the council and the college are canonically independent entities, each having its own distinct functions.[38] And it has been further understood that, while it makes good sense to use the presbyteral council as the exclusive pool from which the consultors are initially selected (since the council represents in a special way the entire presbyterate[39]), nevertheless, once chosen as a consultor, a priest then becomes a member of an entirely distinct body and enjoys a term of office as a consultor that is quite independent of his term of office as a member of the presbyteral council.

There has never been an objective doubt about this matter. Nor has there been an objective doubt about the fact that the bishop is only obliged to replace a consultor when his failure to do so would result in there being less than six consultors in the college. Both of these responses are SIMPLE DECLARATIVE responses.

---

[38]For the functions of the presbyteral council see canons 461 §1; 495 §1; 500 §2; 515 §2; 531; 536 §1; 1215 §2; 1222 §2 and 1263. For the functions of the college of consultors see canons 272; 377 §3; 382 §3; 404 §§1 and 3; 413 §2; 419; 421 §1; 422; 485; 494 §§1 and 2; 501 §2; 833, 4°; 1018 §1, 2°; 1277 and 1292 §1.

[39]Canon 495, §1.

4. A Conference of Bishops' Need for Authorization in order to Issue a General Executory Decree

The Doubt: Whether the expression "general decrees" in canon 455, §1 also includes general executory decrees of the sort in canons 31-33.

The Response: Affirmative.[40]

Canon 455, §1 says that: "a conference of bishops can issue general decrees only in those cases in which either the common law prescribes it[41] or a special mandate of the Apostolic See determines it."

Prior to the response from the Code Commission a doubt existed as to whether this authorization (either by law or mandate) was required only for general *legislative* decrees or for general *executory* decrees as well. A general *legislative* decree may be defined as a common prescription issued by a competent legislator for a community capable of receiving a law, whereas a general *executory* decree is a decree that either determines more precisely the methods to be observed in applying the law, or urges the observance of a law.[42]

Why the doubt? The doubt comes from the fact that the Code never refers to general legislative decrees as general legislative decrees. Rather it always calls them simply "general decrees."[43]   As a result, the term "general decree" becomes ambiguous. One is not sure whether it is a generic term that includes both legislative and executory decrees, or whether it is a specific term that refers only to legislative decrees.

When, therefore, canon 455, §1 said that a conference needed authorization

---

[40]*AAS* 77 (1985) 771; *Periodica* 74 (1985) 609-616.

[41]As, for example, in canon 538, §3 where a conference is expected to issue norms regarding suitable support and housing for a retired pastor; or as in canon 1126 where a conference is expected to establish the way in which the promises in a mixed marriage are to be made, how they are to be established in the external forum and how the non-Catholic party is to be informed of them.

[42]In terms of the examples given in footnote 41, when a conference issues norms in accord with canon 538, §3, that constitutes a general *legislative* decree, whereas when a conference issues norms in accord with canon 1126, that constitutes a general *executory* decree.

[43]See canon 29. The adjective *legislativa* is used in the Code of Canon Law only to modify the noun *potestas*. See Xaverius Ochoa, *Index Verborum ac Locutionum Codicis Iuris Canonici*, (Roma: Commentarium pro Religiosis, 1983) 236.

in order to issue a general decree, it was unclear whether the phrase "general decree" was being used in its generic sense to include both legislative and executory decrees or in its specific sense to refer only to legislative decrees.

Prior to the response from the Code Commission, those who were of the opinion that a conference needed authorization only for the issuance of general legislative decrees, offered the following reasons for their position: a) Since the term "general decree" is defined or described in canon 29 as referring only to general legislative decrees, it must mean the same thing in canon 455, §1; b) Issuing a general executory decree (which simply urges the observance of some law or determines more precisely the ways or circumstances in which that law is to be applied) would seem to be within the proper pastoral competence of a conference of bishops, and should not therefore need any special authorization; and c) Since canon 455, §1 "restricts the free exercise of rights" on the part of a conference, it is, according to canon 18, subject to a strict interpretation, and applies, therefore, only to general legislative decrees.

As weighty and impressive as these arguments are, they are probably not sufficient to constitute an objective doubt. I say this for two reasons: a) A general executory decree is a general decree; and b) Given the general wariness with which Rome has viewed conferences of bishops, it is probably to be expected that the legislator wished to issue authorizations even for general executory decrees.

Since, therefore, we are dealing with only subjective doubt, and since, according to the response, canon 455, §1 would include not just legislative but also executory decrees, I would consider this response to be QUASI-EXTENSIVE.

5. The Non Voting Status of A Superior

The Doubt: Whether, when the law requires that the superior must have the consent of the council or of a body of persons in order to act, in keeping with canon 127, §1, the superior has the right of voting with the others, at least to break a tie.

The Response: Negative.[44]

It is generally understood in law that a superior cannot give advice or consent to him or herself. When, therefore, the law states that a superior may place a certain act only after he or she has obtained the consent of some group, there are then two separate entities involved: the group and the superior; and there are two separate acts involved: first the consent of the group and then the placing of the act by the superior.

A diocesan bishop, for example, although he presides over his college of consultors,[45] is nevertheless distinct from it, and is not a voting member of it. The following case illustrates the principle: a bishop wishes to alienate church property whose value is between the minimum and maximum limits determined by the conference of bishops. In order to do that he needs, in accord with canon 1292, §1, the consent of the college of consultors. This means that more than half the voting members of that group must vote in favor of the alienation in order for the bishop to proceed. The bishop himself does not enjoy a vote in that body, even to break a tie, since he is not a member of the body.

All this is clear and beyond question. But if it is so clear, why then was the question posed to the Code Commission? The question was posed, it seems, because there are, in fact, occasions in the law where the superior acts not as a person *separate from* the council but rather collegially, *along with* the council. There is only one instance of this in the Code itself, and that has to do with the dismissal of a religious from an institute, where canon 699, §1 specifically directs the supreme moderator "to proceed collegially" with the council. But there are other examples in constitutions of particular institutes, which have been approved by the Holy See, where the superior and the council are allowed to act collegially.

---

[44]*AAS* 77 (1985) 771; *Periodica* 74 (1985) 617-623.
[45]Canon 502, §2.

This procedure muddies the waters somewhat in that it appears to expand the council to include the superior. In fact, however, the doubt as posed to the Code Commission envisions a specific case that is quite different from that of canon 699, §1 and other similar arrangements found in particular constitutions. The doubt posed to the Commission deals only with those cases where the superior needs the consent of some group in order to act. And within that context, the principle remains crystal clear: the superior is not a member, certainly not a voting member of the group whose prior consent is needed in order for the superior to act.

The response of the Commission is, therefore, a SIMPLE DECLARATIVE one.

6. The Inability of a Diocesan Bishop to Dispense Outside the Danger of Death from Canonical Form in the Marriage of Two Catholics

The Doubt: Whether outside the case of urgent danger of death the diocesan bishop can dispense according to canon 87, §1 from the canonical form for the marriage of two Catholics.

The Response: Negative.[46]

Canon 1127, §2 allows a local ordinary to dispense from the form of marriage where one party is non-Catholic; canon 1079, §1 allows the local ordinary to dispense from the form of marriage even where both parties are Catholic but only in danger of death; and canon 1165, §2 (with cc. 1161, §1 and 1163, §1) allows the diocesan bishop, after the fact, to sanate a marriage of two Catholics which was invalid because of lack of form.

None of these canons, however, allows the diocesan bishop to dispense two Catholics from the form before the fact and outside the danger of death. The question posed to the Commission was whether he could do that by reason of canon 87, §1, which reads as follows: "As often as he judges that a dispensation will contribute to the spiritual good of the faithful, the diocesan bishop can dispense from both universal and particular disciplinary laws established for his territory or for his subjects by the supreme authority of the Church. He cannot dispense, however, from procedural or penal laws or from those laws whose dispensation is especially reserved to the Apostolic See or to another authority."

Since the form of marriage is not a procedural or penal law but a disciplinary one, there is no problem with the bishop dispensing from it as far as the nature of the law is concerned. The only question then is whether the form of marriage is one of "those laws whose dispensation is especially reserved to the Apostolic See."

Prior to the Code Commission's response, the answer, it would seem, was that the form of marriage is not one of those laws. The Code of Canon Law, at least, does not explicitly list the form of marriage as a law that is reserved to the Apostolic See. The Code lists many other laws that are reserved, among them being mergers and unions of institutes of consecrated life,[47]

[46]*AAS* 77 (1985) 771; *Periodica* 74 (1985) 624-628.
[47]Canon 582.

approving new forms of consecrated life,[48] the granting of an indult to a professed member of an institute of pontifical right to leave the institute,[49] dispensing from the age requirement for the ordination to the presbyterate of one under the age of twenty-four,[50] several irregularities and impediments to receiving orders,[51] certain marriage impediments,[52] the reduction of Mass obligations,[53] and certain excommunications.[54] But nowhere does the Code explicitly indicate that a dispensation from the form of marriage for two Catholics, before the fact and outside the danger of death, is reserved to the Holy See.

Nevertheless the Code Commission has, in effect, ruled that such a dispensation is, in fact, so reserved. The reason for the Commission's ruling, furthermore, seems to be a fairly compelling one. It is this: that throughout the process of drafting the new Code, it was always *understood* by the drafting Commission that such a dispensation was reserved to the Apostolic See. Indeed, the matter, it seems, was settled once and for all in early 1971. At a meeting of the *de matrimonio* coetus held on February 12, 1971, while the group was discussing the present canon 1127, §2, one of the consultors wished the canon to allow the local ordinary to dispense from the form not just in mixed marriages but for the marriages of two Catholics as well. The secretary, however, pointed out that the Holy Father had reserved that dispensation to himself when he issued *De Episcoporum muneribus* in 1966,[55] and that was the end of it. The matter was never discussed again.

It is clear, therefore, that as far as the drafters of the law were concerned, it was accepted that this dispensation was indeed reserved to the Apostolic See. It was never a matter of objective doubt, and the response of the Commission, therefore, is not really restrictive but rather QUASI-RESTRICT-IVE.

---

[48]Canon 605.
[49]Canon 691.
[50]Canon 1031, §4.
[51]Canon 1047, §2.
[52]Canon 1078, §2.
[53]Canon 1308.
[54]Canons 1367; 1370; 1378; 1382 and 1388.
[55]*Communicationes* VIII (1976) 65.

22

7. The Consent for Competence is to be Given by the Judicial Vicar of the Diocese where the Respondent has a Domicile

The Doubt: Whether the judicial vicar whose consent is required according to the norm of canon 1673, 3° is the judicial vicar of the diocese in which the respondent has a domicile, or the judicial vicar of the interdiocesan tribunal.

The Response: Affirmative to the first and "ad mentem." The mind of the legislator is that if in a particular case there is no diocesan judicial vicar, the consent of the bishop is required.[56]

Canon 1673, 3° reads as follows: "In cases regarding the nullity of marriage which are not reserved to the Apostolic See the following are competent: 3° the tribunal of the place in which the petitioner has a domicile, provided that both parties live in the territory of the same conference of bishops and the judicial vicar of the domicile of the respondent agrees, after hearing the respondent."

The question is, what does the phrase "the judicial vicar of the domicile of the respondent" mean? Let us suppose that in a certain province consisting of five dioceses, each of the five dioceses has its own tribunal for nonmatrimonial cases but that, besides those, there is also a provincial tribunal which is exclusively competent to hear in first instance all the matrimonial cases in the entire province. Canon 1673, of course, deals only with marriage cases. When, in the situation described, the consent of the judicial vicar of the domicile of the respondent is required, which judicial vicar is it — the one in charge of all matrimonial cases for the province, or the one who has no jurisdiction over marriage cases but who *is* the judicial vicar of the diocese where the respondent has a domicile?

Clearly it is the latter, since, according to canon 102, §1, a respondent may have a diocesan but not an interdiocesan domicile. The words of the law are *in se certa* — "certain in themselves." The response is a SIMPLE DECLARATIVE one.

---

[56]*AAS* 78 (1986) 1323; *Periodica* 77 (1988) 162-167.

8. The Need for Confirmation Prior to Notification of Dismissal. Recourse against Dismissal is to the Congregation for Religious

I. The Doubt: Whether a dismissed member should be notified of the decree of dismissal, issued in accord with canon 700 by the supreme moderator, before confirmation by the Holy See or only after confirmation.

The Response: Negative to the first part; affirmative to the second.

II. The Doubt: Whether the authority competent to receive the suspensive recourse against the dismissal of a member is the Congregation for Religious and Secular Institutes, which confirmed the decree, or the Supreme Tribunal of the Apostolic Signatura.

The Response: Affirmative to the first part; negative to the second.[57]

In the three years or so before the promulgation of the 1983 Code, canon 700 underwent several changes, not just in its wording but in its very meaning and substance. While it is no doubt true that those changes created the confusion that prompted the first of the doubts stated above, it is also true that a careful reading of the changes holds the key to understanding both the problem and the response to it by the Commission.

Between April 1980 and January 1983 the present canon 700 went through five stages:

Stage 1. When the coetus working on the revision of religious law met to discuss this canon on April 28 - 29, 1980, the question was not so much whether confirmation by the Holy See should come before or after notifying a member of an institute of pontifical right of his or her dismissal; at that point, the question was a more basic one, namely whether there had to be a confirmation by Rome at all. And even on that point the consultors could not agree. Accordingly they wrote alternative canons. Alternative A did not require confirmation, so once the decree of dismissal was issued, the member was so notified and at the same time was apprised of the right to have recourse against the decree to the Holy See. Alternative B, on the other hand, did require confirmation by the Holy See but also noted that, prior to the confirmation, the member should be apprised of the decision to dismiss and be provided the opportunity to present a defense. Each alternative had

[57]*AAS* 78 (1986) 1323; *Periodica* 77 (1988) 149-158.

its adherents. When the matter came to a vote on April 28, five consultors voted in favor of Alternative A, and five voted in favor of Alternative B. It was a deadlock.[58]

Stage 2. Only two months later, on June 29, 1980, the draft of the Code appeared as a schema reserved for the Fathers of the Commission. Canon 626 of that draft, the forerunner to our canon 700, rejected Alternative B and settled on Alternative A. No mention was made of any confirmation by Rome, only the right to recourse.

Stage 3. The *Relatio* of July 16, 1981, that synthesis of animadversions on the 1980 draft of the Code prepared for the Fathers of the Commission who were to meet in plenary session in October 1981, noted that one of the Fathers felt that, in order to protect adequately the rights of the member being dismissed, a confirmation by Rome was essential. He was, in other words, favoring Alternative B. The response was that from the point of view of both procedure and protection of rights, Alternative A was the better approach; nevertheless, the matter would be presented to the Fathers at their plenary meeting in October.[59]

Stage 4. At the plenary meeting, the Fathers voted 36-19 in favor of Alternative B.[60]

Stage 5. Finally the 1983 Code itself retained Alternative B, requiring a confirmation, but with a major difference. Whereas the original Alternative B ordered notification prior to confirmation, the new Alternative B, i.e., canon 700, dropped that requirement and spoke instead of the member's right to recourse.[61]

To those who had followed closely the whole process, it was clear at that point what canon 700 had done: it had accepted the need for confirmation

---

[58]*Communicationes* XIII (1981) 356-358.

[59]*Communicationes* XV (1983) 79.

[60]*Congregatio Plenaria*, Pontificium Consilium De Legum Textibus Interpretandis (Città del Vaticano: Typis Polyglottis Vaticanis, 1991) 286-287.

[61]Canon 700 reads as follows: A decree of dismissal does not take effect unless it has been confirmed by the Holy See to whom the decree and all the acts are to be transmitted; if it is a question of an institute of diocesan right, the confirmation belongs to the bishop of the diocese where the house to which the religious is assigned is situated. The decree, for validity, must indicate the right which the dismissed religious enjoys to have recourse to competent authority within ten days from receiving the notification. The recourse has a suspensive effect.

but rejected the idea of prior notification. Henceforth, according to the canon, the chronology would be: first the issuance of the decree, then the confirmation process, next the notification and finally recourse.

So much for the first doubt. The second flows from it. The question basically is whether recourse against a dismissal is to the Congregation or to the Signatura. The traditional practice as we know, based on canon 1601 of the 1917 Code and canon 1400, §2 of the 1983 Code, is that recourse against an administrative act at this level is to the Congregation. In this particular case, however, there appears to be a problem with that procedure in that it expects the Congregation for Religious to sit in impartial judgment on the legality, merits and justice of a decree which it has itself only recently confirmed.

In its response, the Code Commission, presuming apparently that the Congregation is quite capable of solving the problem, perhaps by making some internal adjustments, has ruled in favor of using the standard procedure in this as in other matters.

Both responses of the Commission are, quite clearly, SIMPLE DECLARA-TIVE ones.

9. A Religious Bishop Lacks Active and Passive Voice in His Own Institute

The Doubt: Whether a religious bishop enjoys active and passive voice in his own institute.

The Response: Negative.[62]

Canon 629, §2 of the 1917 Code specifically noted that a religious bishop who had *retired* as bishop could reside at any of his institute's houses he chose but that he would lack both active voice (the right to vote) and passive voice (eligibility for office).[63] The old Code, however, did not say whether religious bishops while still *active* as bishops, also lacked active and passive voice, and this always remained a disputed question. Woywood-Smith offered the following comment on this question:

> Commentators discuss the question whether the religious who are cardinals and bishops, vicars or prefects apostolic, etc., can have active or passive vote while they are outside the religious organization. On the one hand, they remain religious, as canon 627 states, and there is no express prohibition in the Code against their voting; on the other hand, it seems illogical to say that they can have this power while they are outside the organization, when the Code states that those who return to the community cannot have active or passive vote.[64]

While the former Code was still in effect, the Code Commission never settled the question. There were good arguments and distinguished authorities on both sides. It was probably a matter of objective doubt, so if the Commission had addressed the question, the response would have been either extensive or restrictive, depending on how the Commission ruled, and not just quasi-extensive or quasi-restrictive.

At any rate, when on April 30, 1980 the coetus working on religious law turned its attention to the revision of canon 629 regarding retired religious bishops, it was decided to drop altogether the phrase *sed caret voce activa et*

---

[62]*AAS* 78 (1986) 1324; *Periodica* 77 (1988) 158-162.

[63]It bears noting, incidentally, that in 1975, at the request of the Minister General of the O.F.M. Conventual, the Congregation for Religious and Secular Institutes granted for six years to the retired bishops and prelates of the Order the right to active and passive voice in derogation of canon 629, §2. See *CLD* 9: 453.

[64]Stanislaus Woywood and Callistus Smith, *A Practical Commentary on the Code of Canon Law* (New York: Wagner, 1946) I, 275.

passiva. Instead, said the Commission, the matter would be left up to the law of particular communities.[65] This signified a relaxation from the old law,[66] but more important, it was a clear statement by the Commission that it did not intend to issue universal legislation on this matter. The directive, furthermore, was observed. Neither the comparable canon in the June 1980 draft of the Code (c. 633) nor the one in the 1983 Code (c. 707) said anything at all about active or passive voice for *retired* religious bishops. Nor was anything said in either the 1980 draft or the 1983 Code about active or passive voice for *active* religious bishops. The Code, in other words, is silent on the matter. There is no law whatsoever in the 1983 Code that says anything at all about the right to a voice by a religious bishop.

Indeed, based on the April 30, 1980 directive of the Commission, this appears to be precisely what was intended, namely that nothing be said on the matter in the universal law but that it be left entirely to particular law.

But then along comes the Code Commission and rules that no religious bishop, either retired or active, enjoys a voice. On May 17, 1986, Pope John Paul II ordered the response published but not with any specific approbation, and yet the response does not appear to be an interpretation of a law at all because there is no law. The response rather seems to be a new law, and therefore an ULTRA-RESTRICTIVE "interpretation."[67]

[65]*Communicationes* XIII (1981) 364.

[66]In the spirit, perhaps, of the 1975 grant mentioned in footnote 63.

[67]Perhaps an argument could be made that the Commission's response is in some way based on the phrase in canon 705 which says that a religious bishop "is, in virtue of his vow of obedience, subject to the Roman Pontiff alone," but it is hard to imagine that that phrase could be interpreted to mean that a retired religious bishop, for example, who is back living in the community, does not have a right to vote in the community.

10. The Possibility, after Peremption or Renunciation, of Opening a Case in a Different Court

The Doubt: Whether, when an instance is finished through peremption or by renunciation, if someone wishes to introduce or pursue the cause again, it must be resumed in the forum where it was first treated, or whether it may be introduced before another tribunal which is competent in law at the time of the resumption.

The Response: Negative to the first part; affirmative to the second.[68]

Canon 1741 of the 1917 Code and canon 1525 of the 1983 Code note that renunciation has the same effects regarding the acts as peremption.

Regarding peremption, canon 1522 of the 1983 Code, which repeats virtually verbatim canon 1738 of the former Code, reads as follows: "Peremption extinguishes the acts of the process, but not the acts of the case, which in fact may be operative in another instance provided that the case involves the same persons and the same issue; as regards outsiders the acts of the case have no other value than that of documents."

Both Codes, in other words, say that the fact that an instance has been either perempted or renounced, does not mean that the case can never be heard again. On the contrary, they specifically indicate that, in effect, the action *may* be pursued "provided that (*dummodo*) the case involves the same persons and the same issue." It is significant, of course, that neither the old canon nor the new canon added to that *dummodo* clause the words "and that it be brought before the same tribunal."

A few commentators on the 1917 Code held the position that those words *should* have been added. Sipos, for example, wrote "Even though the instance has been perempted, the action remains and the parties can begin a new instance before the same judge,"[69] but he gave no reasons whatsoever for requiring that it be before the same judge. Most of the commentators, meanwhile, seem to have ignored the question, probably for two reasons: first, that the Code did not require that a perempted or renounced case be reopened before the same tribunal, and secondly because, from a practical point of view, it often makes good sense to reopen a perempted or renounced

---

[68]*AAS* 78 (1986) 1324; *Periodica* 77 (1988) 168-173.

[69]Stephanus Sipos, *Enchiridion Iuris Canonici* (Romae: Herder, 1954) n. 196.

case before a *new* tribunal. Take, for example, the following case: Two young people from Great Britain, while working in New York, fall in love and decide to marry. They return home for the wedding and are married in London. They honeymoon in Italy and from there fly directly back to New York where they continue to work and reside. After a few years they divorce. The woman petitions the New York tribunal to declare the marriage null on the ground of the respondent's intention *contra bonum sacramenti*. She had heard that, prior to marriage, the respondent had told his two closest friends, who are also British citizens living in New York, that he intended to obtain a divorce if the marriage didn't work out. When, however, the New York tribunal cites the respondent and the two witnesses, they all decline to participate in the proceedings, and the case ends by peremption.

Over the next five years the two parties as well as the two witnesses all leave New York and return to live in England. The respondent and witnesses, moreover, indicate that they would now be willing to testify before a church tribunal, so the woman decides to reopen the case. It would obviously make little sense for her to reopen the case in New York which not only lacks any present competence to hear the case but also lacks any real facility to hear the testimony of the respondent and witnesses. It clearly makes much more sense to reopen the case in a competent tribunal in England.

This common sense solution is, indeed, the approach taken by the Code Commission whose response on the issue is a SIMPLE DECLARATIVE one.

11. The Applicability of Canon 1103 on Force and Fear to Non-Catholics

The Doubt: Whether the defect of consent referred to in canon 1103 can be applied to marriages of non-Catholics.

The Response: Affirmative.[70]

Since the Middle Ages it has been debated among canonists and theologians whether force and fear is a matrimonial "impediment" of the natural law or only of ecclesiastical law. If it were of the natural law then it would apply to the marriages of non-Catholics, but if it were of only ecclesiastical law it would not.

Following the ruling of the Code Commission that canon 1103 can be applied to the marriages of non-Catholics, Urban Navarrete, S.J. published a fourteen page commentary on the Commission's response.[71] Navarrete's position was, in effect, that the response was ultra-extensive. Navarrete took this position, it seems, for two basic reasons. First, because, as a question that had been debated for several hundred years and never definitively settled, the matter was a doctrinal, not a canonical one. Any response, therefore, was within the competence of the Congregation for the Doctrine of the Faith, and beyond the competence of the Code Commission. Secondly, the fact is, according to Navarrete, that the wording of canon 1103 contains elements of both the natural law and ecclesiastical law,[72] so it is an oversimplification on the Commission's part to say that the canon can be applied as is to the marriages of non-Catholics. In point of fact, says Navarrete, judges must, in individual cases, exercise extreme diligence to make sure that they apply to the marriages of non-Catholics only those elements of canon 1103 which are truly of the natural law.

My own position regarding this response of the Commission is quite different. It seems to me that the Second Vatican Council did, in fact, definitively settle the question in favor of the Thomistic position that fear invalidates marriage by reason of the natural law itself. Several citations from the Council could be made, but suffice it to note here that number 29 of

---

[70]*AAS* 79 (1987) 1132.

[71]*Periodica* 77 (1988) 497-510. For an English translation of Navarrete's commentary plus some concluding observations of my own, see "Urban Navarrete, S.J. and the Response of the Code Commission on Force and Fear," *The Jurist* 51 (1991) 119-137.

[72]According to Navarrete, for example, indirect fear, that is to say, fear that is not inflicted for the purpose of extorting consent, does not easily appear to be an element of the natural law.

Gaudium et spes refers to the faculty of freely choosing a spouse as a "fundamental right" of both women and men. Now a fundamental right comes from the natural law, so it seems clear that, by those words, the Council was endorsing the position that force and fear is of the natural law.

The response of the Code Commission was, therefore, a simple and rather obvious canonical application of a theoretical position which, by the close of Vatican II, had become certain doctrine. I see the response, therefore, as a SIMPLE DECLARATIVE one.

12. The Right of Different Ordinaries to Prescribe the Purposes for Which Stipends Offered for Binated and Trinated Masses May Be Used

The Doubt: Whether the ordinary referred to in canon 951, §1 ought to be understood as the ordinary of the place where the Mass is celebrated or as the proper ordinary of the celebrant.

The Response: Negative to the first part; affirmative to the second, except for a pastor or parochial vicar in which case the ordinary of the place shall be understood.[73]

Canon 951, §1 reads as follows: "A priest who celebrates Mass more than once on the same day may apply the individual Mass for the intention for which the offering is made, but with the law that, except on Christmas, he may retain the offering for only one Mass, giving the other offerings to purposes prescribed by the ordinary, except for some recompense by reason of an extrinsic title."

The question posed to the Commission regarding this canon is of practical importance for religious institutes or societies of apostolic life of pontifical right. The major superiors of such institutes and societies are, in accord with canon 134, §1, ordinaries. Imagine, for example, a diocese in which Dominican priests not only staff a parish but also administer and teach at a college. When those Dominican priests binate or trinate, who has the right of determining the ultimate recipient of the offering for the second and third Masses? Is it the ordinary of the place (in practice, the diocesan bishop) or is it their own ordinary (i.e., the Dominican provincial or Master General)?

The response of the Commission was clear. For the pastor and the parochial vicars, it is the ordinary of the place, but for all others it is their own ordinary who makes the determination.

The only question then is whether, prior to the response, the meaning of canon 951, §1 was certain in itself or whether it was objectively doubtful. A brief history of the canon answers that question:

1917 - Canon 824, §2 did not allow a priest to accept more than one stipend a day.

---

[73]*AAS* 79 (1987) 1132; *Periodica* 77 (1988) 511-518.

1974 - On June 13, 1974, Pope Paul VI issued the motu proprio *Firma in traditione* in which, under III a, he allowed that a priest could accept more than one stipend a day, but noted that the stipend for the second and third Mass "must be expended on needs specified by the diocesan bishop."[74] At that point, therefore, it was only the diocesan bishop who could make the determination.

1975 - Canon 111, §2 of the 1975 schema on the sacraments (an early version of the present c. 951, §2) said that the stipends offered for the second and third Masses could not be retained by the priest but should "accrue to the good of the Church, according to the prescriptions of the ordinary of the place." So it is still not the ordinary but the ordinary of the place who makes the determination.[75]

1975 - On November 4, 1975, the Congregation for Religious granted a rescript to the Dominican Master General, extending for two years a faculty originally granted in 1970, allowing Dominican priests "to accept stipends for binated and trinated Masses to meet the needs of the provinces and missions."[76] For the Dominicans, therefore, it was no longer the ordinary of the place but their own ordinary who by special rescript, would make the determination.

1977 - On October 17, 1977, the Congregation for Religious renewed for three years the 1975 rescript to the Dominicans but now added the following restriction: "excluded are pastors and vice pastors in the strict sense, if the ordinary of the place so requires."[77]

1978 - When the coetus working on sacramental law met in October of 1978 to discuss, among other subjects, the matter of stipends, it was decided, no doubt in light of these and other similar rescripts, to change the wording of the canon from "ordinary of the place" to simply "ordinary." And so the canon remained from then until the final promulgation of the Code.

It is clear, therefore, that the choice of the term "ordinary" was no accident but rather the final step in an evolutionary process. It is clear, furthermore, that the drafters of the Code understood the term "ordinary" to mean the

---

[74]*CLD* 8, 532.
[75]*Communicationes* XIII (1981) 433.
[76]*CLD* 9, 588-589.
[77]Ibid.

presider's ordinary unless, in accord with the 1977 rescript, the priest was a pastor or parochial vicar, in which case it would be the ordinary of the place. The response, therefore, was a SIMPLE DECLARATIVE one.

13. Religious in Both Perpetual and Temporary Vows May Transfer from One Monastery to Another within the Same Institute

The Doubt: Whether by the term "religious" in canon 684, §3 is to be understood only religious in perpetual vows or also religious in temporary vows.

The Response: Negative to the first, affirmative to the second.[78]

The first three paragraphs of canon 684 read as follows:

§1. A member in perpetual vows cannot transfer from one religious institute to another without the permission of the supreme moderator of each institute given with the consent of their respective councils.

§2. After completing a probationary period which is to last at least three years, the member can be admitted to perpetual profession in the new institute. However, if the member refuses to make this profession or is not admitted to making it by competent superiors, the member is to return to the former institute, unless an indult of secularization has been obtained.

§3. For a religious to transfer from an autonomous monastery to another of the same institute or federation or confederation, it is required and is sufficient to have the consent of the major superior of both monasteries and the chapter of the receiving monastery, with due regard for other requirements determined in proper law; a new profession is not required.

The basic question here is whether a religious in temporary vows should be permitted to transfer from one monastery to another within the same institute, e.g., from one Benedictine monastery to another.

There is one rather obvious problem with permitting one in temporary vows to transfer. As Elizabeth McDonough puts it:

. . . the requirements of probation coupled with the ordinary requirements for temporary profession (cc. 655 and 657) make it very likely that temporary profession would expire during the time of probation. In such a case it is not very reasonable to expect to be admitted to renewal of vows in a community from which one is seeking transfer, and it is not legally possible to pronounce vows before completion of probation in the

---

[78]*AAS* 79 (1987) 1249; *Periodica* 78 (1989) 143-153.

community to which one is seeking transfer.[79]

With this and other difficulties in mind, the coetus which was putting this canon into its final form in 1980 voted overwhelmingly to disallow temporary professed from any transfer and to permit transfer only for those in perpetual vows. This is absolutely clear from the minutes of the coetus' meeting on March 3, 1980. The task of the coetus that day was, in terms of this canon, to revise the emended text of the 1977 draft canon. In this canon's paragraph 3, members in temporary vows were allowed to transfer provided that they repeated the novitiate and then made a temporary profession of at least three years. When the coetus finished its work on the canon and, in effect, produced a draft canon (which the present c. 684 repeats virtually verbatim), it was no doubt satisfied that it had succeeded in expressing clearly that only those in perpetual vows would be permitted to transfer from institute to institute or from monastery to monastery.

In order to accomplish that, the coetus took the following actions: a) for the explicit purpose of "restricting transfer only to the perpetual professed," it suppressed the old paragraph 3 altogether;[80] b) where paragraph 1 of the 1977 draft had spoken only of a "member," the coetus added the words "in perpetual vows";[81] and c) it added the notion that when transferring from one monastery to another a new profession would not be required.[82]

The mind of the coetus was, therefore, clear: all transfers would be restricted to those in perpetual vows. Nevertheless, the actual wording of canon 684, §3, which speaks only of "a religious" and not of "a religious in perpetual vows" amounts to a kind of loophole, and it was this *lacuna* that gave rise to the doubt posed to the Code Commission.

Given the drafting history of this canon, one would have expected the Commission to have responded in a manner diametrically opposed to the way it in fact did. Presumably, after all, the mind of the coetus is the mind of the legislator, but now we have an authentic interpretation which states, in effect,

---

[79]Elizabeth McDonough, O.P., "Separation of Members from the Institute: Canons 684-709," in *A Handbook on Canons 573-746*, edited by Jordan Hite, Sharon Holland, and Daniel Ward (Collegeville: The Liturgical Press, 1985) 230.

[80]*Communicationes* XIII (1981) 328 under proposition 6.

[81]Ibid.

[82]Ibid. Under proposition 11. Obviously, if those in temporary vows were permitted to transfer, then a new profession *would* be required in order for the person to continue to be a religious.

that, in this particular case, the mind of the legislator is exactly the opposite of the mind of the coetus.

How then should the interpretation be classified? Since the very coetus that drafted the law was in agreement that only those in perpetual vows could transfer, that position was surely a solidly probable one at the very least, and enjoyed the status of constituting, again at the very least, an objective doubt. The response of the Commission, therefore, is explanatory and not declarative. But is it simple explanatory or extensive? An argument could certainly be made, based on the drafting history and the sense of the entire canon, that the interpretation is extensive. But, on the other hand, the term "religious" is a generic one which, in general, includes all religious, i.e., those in both perpetual and temporary vows. Thus it would be difficult to say that the Commission's response is really extending the term beyond its ordinary meaning. I would therefore classify the response as a SIMPLE EXPLANATORY one.[83]

---

[83]When all is said and done, does this response raise the further question as to whether temporary professed may transfer not only from monastery to monastery within the same institute, but even from institute to institute?

14. An Imprimatur Is To Be Printed in the Book Itself

The Doubt: Whether the permission which is mentioned in canon 830, §3 is to be printed in published books, indicating the name of the one giving the permission, the date and place of the grant of permission.

The Response: Affirmative.[84]

Canon 830 reads as follows:

§1. The conference of bishops can compile a list of censors known for their knowledge, correct doctrine and prudence who could aid diocesan curias, or it can establish a commission of censors which local ordinaries can consult; however, the right of each local ordinary to entrust the judging of books to persons approved by him still remains intact.

§2. In undertaking the office, the censor, laying aside any respect for persons, is to consider only the teaching of the Church concerning faith and morals as it is proposed by the ecclesiastical magisterium.

§3. The censor's opinion must be given in writing; if it is favorable, the ordinary, in his own prudent judgment, is to grant the permission to publish, giving his own name and the time and place of the granting of the permission; if, however, he does not grant the permission, the ordinary is to communicate the reasons for his refusal to the author of the work.

The meaning of the phrase "giving his own name and the time and place of the granting of the permission" in §3 is unclear. Does it mean that the ordinary gives his name, etc., in the decree granting the permission or does it mean that it should be printed in the book itself?

The parallel canon in the 1917 Code, canon 1394, §1, stated explicitly that the imprimatur should be printed "in the beginning or end of the book." Canon 830, §3, however, is not so much an updating of the former canon 1394, §1 as it is an almost (but not quite) verbatim repetition of Article 6, n. 3 of *Ecclesiae pastorum*, the 1975 decree issued by the Congregation for the Doctrine of the Faith on "the vigilance of the Church's pastors regarding books."[85]

---

[84]*AAS* 79 (1987) 1249; *Periodica* 17 (1988) 625-628.
[85]*AAS* 67 (1975) 281, 284; *CLD* 8: 991-996.

Although the differences between *Ecclesiae pastorum* and canon 830, §3 are slight, the former was clearer on this point. Instead of saying, as the canon does, that the ordinary "is to grant the permission to publish, giving his own name", etc., *Ecclesiae pastorum* said that the ordinary "is to grant the permission to publish with his approbation, giving his own name", etc. By omitting the words "with his approbation" the canon lost some clarity and left the reader wondering whether the imprimatur had to be printed in the book itself.

Nevertheless it seems reasonable to conclude that, when the canon requires the ordinary to give his name as well as the time and place of the grant, it is talking about including those items not just in the decree but in the book itself. Two reasons in particular support this conclusion: a) it goes without saying that the permission should be given in writing and not just orally, and it likewise goes without saying that the document would include the name of the ordinary along with the date and place. Otherwise the author and publisher would have no proof that the imprimatur had ever been granted. It is highly unlikely, therefore, that the Code is merely asking that such obvious information be included in the decree; and b) it is, on the contrary, very likely that the Code is asking that this information be printed in the book itself, since the whole point of the law is to provide a means by which people will be able to identify which books are published with ecclesiastical permission and which are not.

The response of the Code Commission is, therefore, a SIMPLE DECLARATIVE one.

15. The Inability of the Diocesan Bishop to Allow a Layperson To Give a Homily

The Doubt: Whether the diocesan bishop is able to dispense from the prescription of canon 767, §1, by which the homily is reserved to priests and deacons.

The Response: Negative.[86]

Like the sixth response of the Commission (on the inability of the diocesan bishop to dispense from the form of marriage for two Catholics), this response also deals with the dispensing power of the diocesan bishop.

Since canon 87 recognizes the ability of a diocesan bishop to dispense from disciplinary laws that are not specially reserved to the Holy See, and since canon 767, §1 (which reserves the giving of a homily to a priest or deacon) *is* a disciplinary law and one that is not known by anyone to be specially reserved to the Holy See, one wonders why the Code Commission responds to this doubt in the negative rather than in the affirmative. Is it that the Commission is hereby advising us that henceforth a dispensation from this law will be regarded as one that is specially reserved? Perhaps, but if so, this would seem to be the establishment of an entirely new law. Establishing a new law, however, is beyond the ordinary competence of the Commission, and such an "interpretation," therefore, would be ultra-restrictive.

Perhaps then the response of the Commission is based on a source other than canon 87. If so, that other source can only be canon 86, which states that a constitutive law, i.e., a law which defines those elements which essentially constitute an action, is not subject to dispensation. The question then is this: is canon 767, §1 a constitutive law? According to James Provost, one school of thought holds that a homily is not a homily unless it is given by a priest or deacon.[87] According to this school, therefore, canon 767, §1 is a constitutive law in that it identifies delivery by one in holy orders as at least one of the essential elements that constitutes a homily.

Presumably, however, this is not the reason why the Code Commission has

---

[86]*AAS* 79 (1987) 1249; *Periodica* 77 (1988) 613-624.
[87]*Roman Replies and CLSA Advisory Opinions 1986* (Washington: CLSA, 1986) 72. See also Joseph Fox, "The Homily and the Authentic Interpretation of Canon 767, §1," *Apollinaris* 62 (1989) 123-169.

ruled that a diocesan bishop cannot dispense from this canon. Because if it were, the Commission would be saying implicitly that a diocesan bishop can indeed permit laypersons to preach, after the Gospel at Mass, about the mysteries of faith and the norms of Christian life, basing their preaching on the liturgical texts of the day; but what a bishop cannot do is to call that preaching a "homily." This, however, would amount to a kind of semantic legerdemain and is presumably not what the Code Commission was saying.

What then was the Commission's rationale for this response? Perhaps the best clue to that rationale is found in a private response on this question from the President of the Commission, a response which predated by several months the official response here under discussion. In that private response, the President first noted that the matter "will require further research and study following the established procedures of this Commission," but then he went on to offer a personal opinion. He wrote "My own personal opinion about the case you present is that the bishop does not have the power to dispense from the law. This particular canon is not simply a disciplinary law but also a liturgical law. It states that the homily, reserved to a priest or deacon, is some kind of constitutive part of the liturgical celebration."[88]

Although this personal opinion of the Cardinal President is interesting, its meaning is not entirely clear. Presumably the President is not saying that canon 767, §1 is a constitutive law in the sense that a homily is not a homily unless preached by a cleric; nor is he saying that the liturgy of the Eucharist would not be the liturgy of the Eucharist without a homily preached by a cleric, since that is patently untrue. Perhaps then, the sense is this: that just as a diocesan bishop could not permit a layperson to offer the opening prayer at Mass or the prayer over the gifts, so neither could a diocesan bishop permit a person to give the homily. It would seem, however, that the *reason* why a bishop cannot dispense from the liturgical law that requires the priest to offer the prayers at Mass is that the bishop would not have the "just and reasonable cause" which canon 90, §1 requires in order for such a dispensation to be granted validly. This, however, would not necessarily be the case as regards the homily.

Given, therefore, the absence of any clear justification for restricting the right of the diocesan bishop in this matter, I am inclined, pending further

---

[88]*Roman Replies and CLSA Advisory Opinions 1987* (Washington: CLSA, 1987) 6-7. A copy of the original letter in the files of the CLSA shows that the letter was indeed signed by the President and not by the Pro-President as indicated on p. 7 of the 1987 *Roman Replies.*

enlightenment, to agree with the esteemed F. J. Urrutia[89] and conclude that this response of the Code Commission is an ULTRA-RESTRICTIVE one.

[89]*Periodica* 77 (1988) 624.

16. The Inability of Extraordinary Ministers of Holy Communion to Exercise Their Office When Ordinary Ministers are Present and Unimpeded

The Doubt: Whether the extraordinary minister of Holy Communion, deputed in accordance with canons 910, §2 and 230, §3, can exercise his or her supplementary function even when ordinary ministers, who are not in any way impeded, are present in the church, though not taking part in the Eucharistic celebration.

The Response: Negative.[90]

Canon 910, §2 says that "the extraordinary minister of Holy Communion is an acolyte or other member of the Christian faithful deputed in accord with canon 230, §3."

Canon 230, §3 reads as follows:

When the necessity of the Church warrants it and when ministers are lacking, lay persons, even if they are not lectors or acolytes, can also supply for certain of their offices, namely, to exercise the ministry of the word, to preside over liturgical prayers, to confer baptism, and to distribute Holy Communion in accord with the prescriptions of law.

The doubt presented to the Code Commission is this: when canon 230, §3 says that lay persons can distribute Holy Communion only "when ministers are lacking" (*deficientibus ministris*), what does that mean? Can ministers be said to be lacking when, though present in the church, they are not actually taking part in the Eucharistic celebration?

The doubt was, it seems, prompted at least in part by a phrase that appeared in *Inaestimabile donum*, the 1980 instruction from the Congregation for the Sacraments and Divine Worship. After noting that extraordinary ministers of the Eucharist are permitted to distribute communion only when either there is no priest, deacon or acolyte, or the priest is impeded by illness or advanced age, or the number of the faithful going to communion is so large as to make the celebration of Mass excessively long, the instruction then concluded: "To be reprobated therefore is the practice of those priests who, although they are themselves taking part in the celebration (*licet celebrationi*

[90]*AAS* 80 (1988) 1373; *Periodica* 78 (1989) 269-277.

44

ipsi intersint) nevertheless abstain from distributing communion, leaving that task to lay persons."[91]

Since the only practice that was being criticized by the Congregation (if my translation of the word *intersint* is correct) involved priests who were actually taking part in the celebration, the implication seemed to be that priests present in the church but not participating in the Eucharist could legitimately leave the distribution of communion up to the extraordinary ministers. Hence the doubt posed to the Code Commission.

Nevertheless, canon 230, §3 is clear: extraordinary ministers may distribute only when ordinary ministers are "lacking," and according to the standard method of interpreting such phrases, a minister may be either *physically* "lacking" (when absent) or *morally* "lacking" (when impeded). When, therefore, the Commission rules, by this response, that an extraordinary minister may not distribute Holy Communion when an ordinary minister is present and unimpeded, it is giving a SIMPLE DECLARATIVE interpretation.

[91]*AAS* 72 (1980) 336.

17. The Right of Aggrieved Faithful to Hierarchical Recourse Against a Decree of Their Bishop

The Doubt: Whether a group of faithful, lacking juridical personality and even the recognition envisaged in canon 299, §3, can legitimately make hierarchical recourse against a decree of its own diocesan bishop.

The Response: Negative, as a group; in the affirmative, as individual members of the faithful acting either singly or together, provided that they really have a grievance. However, in estimating the grievance, the judge must be allowed suitable discretion.[92]

The nucleus of this response by the Commission seems fairly obvious. It says basically that while a group of faithful lacking juridical personality cannot, precisely as a *group*, make recourse against a decree of their bishop, nevertheless as *individuals*, acting either singly or together, they can. This, however, is but a simple application of canon 310 which reads as follows:

> A private association which has not been constituted a juridic person cannot as such be a subject of obligations and rights; however, the Christian faithful associated together in it can jointly contract obligations and acquire rights and possess goods as co-owners and co-possessors; they can exercise their rights and obligations through an agent or proxy.

The nucleus of the response, therefore, is a simple declarative one. The coda of the response, however, beginning with the words "provided that they really have a grievance" is another matter. Requiring people to show grievance and awarding the judge discretion in estimating the grievance before the right to recourse is recognized, seems to go beyond the requirements of canon 1737, §1, which simply says that "one who claims to have been injured by a decree can make recourse for any just reason to the hierarchic superior of the one who issued the decree."

The obvious difference between canon 1737, §1 and the Commission's response is that the canon only requires that a person *claim* to have been injured or aggrieved in order to make recourse, whereas the response requires that the person *really* have a grievance.

While it may be presumed that the Commission certainly does not intend

---

[92]*AAS* 80 (1988) 1818; *Periodica* 78 (1989) 261-268.

that the matter be judged before the case is accepted, nevertheless the Commission does seem to be endorsing a kind of preliminary screening process in order to determine whether the decree in question injured the person in some way.

Even this preliminary process, however, must be judged to be demanding more than the law itself demands, namely, a) a *claim* of being aggrieved by the decree; and b) a just reason. While it is true that the term "a just reason," when read in light of Article 123, §1 of *Pastor bonus*," would necessarily include a claim that the decree violated some law, nevertheless it is, again, only a *claim* at this point and nothing more.[93]

When, therefore, the response demands a real grievance and not just a claim of grievance, it is not, as I understand it, merely interpreting canon 1737, §1 but going beyond it, and it must therefore be considered ULTRA-RESTRICTIVE.

---

[93]Article 123 §1, speaking of the competence of the Signatura, reads "It also hears recourses filed within the peremptory term of thirty available days against individual administrative acts either handed down or approved by Dicasteries of the Roman Curia, as often as it is claimed that the impugned act violated some law either in deciding or in proceeding." *Communicationes* XX (1988) 44.

For more on this matter see E. Labandeira, "Il Ricorso Gerarchico Canonico: *Petitum e Causa Petendi*," *Ius Ecclesiae* (1991) 103-118 and Joaquin Llobell Tuset, "Il *Petitum e la Causa Petendi* nel Contenzioso - Amministrativo Canonico. Profili Sostanziali Ricostruttivi alla Luce della Cost. Ap. *Pastor Bonus*," *Ius Ecclesiae* (1991) 119-150.

One wonders in the end whether the Code Commission's requirement "that they really have a grievance" applies to all petitioners or only to those members of a group who are petitioning as individual members of the faithful.

18. Those Who Procure an Abortion, either by Ejecting an Immature Fetus or by Killing a Fetus, are Excommunicated

The Doubt: Whether abortion, mentioned in canon 1398, is to be understood only as the ejection of an immature fetus, or also as the killing of the fetus in whatever way it may be procured or at whatever time from the moment of conception.

The Response: Negative to the first part; affirmative to the second.[94]

Traditionally an abortion has been defined as the ejection of a live, immature, i.e., nonviable fetus from the mother's womb. Canon 1398, repeating in substance canon 2350, §1 of the 1917 Code, says that "a person who procures a successful abortion incurs an automatic excommunication."

Feticide is, strictly speaking, different from abortion. Feticide involves the killing of the fetus while it is still in the womb, whereas in abortion the fetus is alive when it is ejected from the womb.

Feticide is a species of homicide, and homicide is not punished by automatic excommunication either in the 1917 Code[95] or in the 1983 Code.[96]

Morally, abortion and feticide would seem to be equally wrong. But there is a canonical question here, and it is this: considering the principle that "laws which establish a penalty are subject to strict interpretation,"[97] are those who commit feticide subject to the same canonical penalty as those who commit abortion?

Traditionally most authors were of the opinion that they are not. Coronata, for example, wrote "Practically all authors, both ancient and more modern, teach that craniotomy and embryotomy do not come under the name of abortion and that those who perform or procure those operations are not subject to the penalties stated in this canon."[98] Nevertheless a few authors, including Coronata himself, were of the opinion that, since feticide is

---

[94]*AAS* 80 (1988) 1818; *Periodica* 78 (1989) 278-286.

[95]Canon 2354.

[96]Canon 1397.

[97]Canon 18 in the new Code; canon 19 in the old.

[98]Matthaeus Conte a Coronata, *Institutiones Iuris Canonici* (Romae: Marietti, 1955) IV, n. 2015.

tantamount to abortion, those who commit feticide would be subject to the same penalty as those who procure an abortion.

When canon 1398 was being considered by the revising coetus in its meeting of April 22, 1977, some asked that a definition of abortion be given. The consultors, however, saw no reason to define abortion because, they said, "Catholic doctrine is clear on this point."[99] One can only conclude that, in making this statement, the consultors were endorsing the traditional definition of abortion as the ejection of a live, immature fetus from the womb, and that very likely, therefore, they were also endorsing the more common opinion that those who commit feticide do not incur automatic excommunication.

Nevertheless, in recent years, most "abortions" have been procured either by suction or by a dilation and curettage or by a prostaglandin drug, often in conjunction with the RU 486 pill, or by saline poisoning. Since, however, in all of these procedures the fetus is usually killed in the womb, such methods are not, strictly speaking, abortions as that term has been traditionally defined.

The Code Commission's decision, therefore, to broaden the definition of abortion (which is, in effect, what this response does) makes eminent sense. Nevertheless, given the history of canon 1398 and the fact that the more common opinion has always held that those who commit feticide do not incur automatic excommunication, this ruling by the Commission, which extends the penalty attached to canon 1398 to include those who have committed feticide, is an EXTENSIVE one, and is not, therefore, retroactive.

---

[99] *Communicationes* IX (1977) 317.

19. Religious Judges on the Roman Rota Are Not Exempt from Their Own Religious Ordinaries or Their Obligations as Religious

The Doubt: Whether religious, appointed judges of the Roman Rota, are to be considered exempt from the religious ordinary and from the obligation deriving from religious profession as in the case of religious raised to the episcopate.

The Response: Negative to both, except in what concerns the exercise of their office.[100]

A long tradition in the Church recognized that religious priests who were named as Rotal auditors were exempt from the jurisdiction of their own religious superiors and also from the obligation of common life and from the vow of poverty to the extent that they judged those obligations to be incompatible with their office as auditor. The historical highlights of that tradition are the following:

a) On July 26, 1913, Pope Pius X recognized as a privilege originally granted to Rotal auditors in 1349 that "they are exempt, by personal immunity, from the jurisdiction of their Ordinaries." This privilege clearly referred not just to diocesan priests but to religious priests as well.[101]

b) The 1917 Code contained a chapter entitled "On the Obligations and Privileges of Religious Promoted to an Ecclesiastical Dignity or in Charge of Parishes."[102] This chapter specifically noted in canon 627 that religious bishops and cardinals were exempt from the jurisdiction of their religious superiors and could make their own prudent judgment about the extent to which they should adhere to the obligations stemming from their religious profession. Although the canon dealt explicitly only with religious bishops and cardinals, nevertheless partly because of the long-standing tradition mentioned by Pius X a few years earlier, partly because of the chapter heading, which referred to religious promoted not just to the episcopate but to any "ecclesiastical dignity," and partly by reason of analogical application, it was generally understood that the same exemptions applied to religious Rotal auditors as well.

---

[100]*AAS* 80 (1988) 1819; *Periodica* 78 (1989) 361-379.

[101]F. X. Wernz, *Ius Decretalium*, (Prati: Propaganda, 1914) V, 75, n. 53, num. 2.

[102]Bk. 2, Part 2, Title 13, Ch. 3 - which includes canons 626-631.

c) When the drafting coetus met on April 29, 1980 and discussed this canon, the secretary noted that "it might be necessary to broaden the sense of canon 627 so that it refers to vicars, prefects apostolic and others mentioned in canon 628," i.e., those raised to an ecclesiastical dignity outside their own institute.[103]

Shortly thereafter, however, it appears that the tide began to turn. When the draft of the whole Code appeared a few months later in June 1980, the chapter heading comparable to the one mentioned above read simply: "On Religious Raised to the Episcopate" with no mention at all of religious raised to other ecclesiastical dignities; and the canon comparable to the old canon 627 (numbered 631) likewise spoke only of religious raised to the episcopate.

Finally the 1983 Code itself retained the same chapter heading as the 1980 draft and the same wording of the canon, now numbered 705.

Two factors in particular seem to lie behind the fact that the 1983 Code no longer extends the exemption to religious Rotal auditors but restricts it to religious bishops. First, that it is fitting that religious bishops, by reason of their special bond of communion with the Roman Pontiff, Head of the College of Bishops, should be subject only to him; and secondly that religious Rotal auditors should follow the directive of *Christus Dominus* 35, 2, which reads: "Religious engaged in the active apostolate, however, should be imbued with the spirit of their religious community, and remain faithful to the observance of their rule and to submissiveness toward their own superiors."

The response of the Commission is a SIMPLE DECLARATIVE one.

---

[103]*Communicationes* XIII (1981) 363. It must be noted, however, that when the Secretary went on to suggest a revised version of the canon, it included vicars and prefects apostolic but did not include those raised to any other ecclesiastical dignity outside their own institute, like, for example, a Rotal auditor. The Secretary's revised version read as follows: "A religious raised to the episcopate or promoted to the leadership of some particular Church, remains a member of his own institute but in virtue of his vow of obedience is subject to the Roman Pontiff alone and is not bound by obligations which he himself prudently judges cannot be reconciled with his position."

20. The Impossibility of an Auxiliary Bishop Being President or Pro-President of a Conference of Bishops or of a Regional Gathering of Bishops

The Doubt: Whether an auxiliary bishop is able to undertake the office of president (or pro-president) of an episcopal conference. Whether he can undertake such a position in gatherings of the bishops of ecclesiastical regions mentioned in canon 434.

The Response: Negative to both.[104]

On March 10, 1989, the President of the Law Council, Cardinal Castillo Lara himself issued a commentary on this response in which he noted that the negative response by the Commission might create some wonderment. First, because in point of fact more than one auxiliary bishop had already been elected as president of a conference (and as the ancient axiom says "Against a fact there is no argument"), and secondly, because the Code does not explicitly forbid an auxiliary bishop from being elected as president of a conference.[105] The pertinent canon, canon 452, reads simply:

Canon 452, §1. Each conference of bishops is to elect a president for itself; it is also to determine who is to serve in the role of pro-president when the president is legitimately impeded; and it is also to appoint a general secretary of the conference, according to the norm of the statutes.

§2. The president of the conference, and the pro-president when the former is legitimately impeded, preside not only at the general meetings of the conference of bishops but also over its permanent council.

Nevertheless in his commentary, Cardinal Castillo Lara offers several compelling reasons for the Commission's ruling. His position may be summarized as follows:

a. *The Nature of the Presidency of a Conference*: The presidency is not an honorary title but a position of great importance. The president, for example, presides over the meetings of the conference and of its permanent council; he acts in the person of the conference, expresses opinions about the mind of the conference, prepares, along with the permanent council, the agenda for the meeting and sees to the implementation of the conference's decisions.

[104]*AAS* 81 (1989) 388; *Periodica* 80 (1991) 107.
[105]*Communicationes* XXI (1989) 94-98.

b. *The Nature of a Conference of Bishops*: Canon 447, which is based on *Christus Dominus* 38,1, notes that the whole point of a conference of bishops is to allow the bishops of a given nation or territory to exercise jointly certain pastoral functions. It is, therefore, the exercise of the pastoral office that is at the heart of a conference.

c. *The Nature of a Diocesan Bishop*: Canon 369 defines a diocese as a portion of the People of God which is entrusted for pastoral care to a bishop with the cooperation of the presbyterate so that, adhering to its pastor and gathered by him in the Holy Spirit through the gospel and the Eucharist, it constitutes a particular church in which the one, holy, catholic and apostolic Church of Christ is truly present and operative.

It is clear from this canon that the special competence of the diocesan bishop is his pastoral office, that there is only one diocesan bishop in a diocese and that collegial leadership in the strict sense is inconceivable.

d. *The Relationship of a Diocesan Bishop to a Conference*: Canon 448, §1 says that "generally the conference of bishops encompasses all who preside over particular churches of the same nation." The natural and proper members of a conference, therefore, are diocesan bishops and those equivalent to them, for only they have a direct, immediate and personal responsibility for a portion of the People of God. The special title, in other words, by which one is a member of a conference is not the episcopal character but the condition of being pastor of a particular church.

e. *The Nature of an Auxiliary Bishop*: The duty of the auxiliary bishop, as the name implies, is to assist and to cooperate with the diocesan bishop. An auxiliary bishop does not enjoy any autonomous pastoral responsibility in a diocese or any jurisdiction except what the diocesan bishop delegates (although as vicar general or vicar episcopal he enjoys ordinary, vicarious jurisdiction).

f. *The Relationship of an Auxiliary Bishop to a Conference*: Canon 454 says that an auxiliary bishop does not, by the law itself, enjoy a deliberative vote in the conference (though he might by the statutes of a particular conference). Since, however, a deliberative vote is the primary right of any member of any collegial group, it is clear that an auxiliary bishop is not a member of a conference by full right but is rather a kind of second grade member.

g. *A Comparison of a Conference with a Plenary Council*: In a plenary council an auxiliary bishop enjoys a deliberative vote (c. 443, §1, 2°) and is therefore a full member, but is still not eligible to be elected as president (c. 441, 3°). This legislation clearly tends to confirm the conclusion that an auxiliary bishop is likewise ineligible for election as president of a conference.

Given Cardinal Castillo Lara's persuasive reasoning in support of the Commission's response, the response, it appears, is not truly restrictive but only QUASI-RESTRICTIVE.

21. The Right of the Diocesan Bishop to Appoint the President of a Chapter of Canons

The Doubt: Whether canon 509, §1 requires that a chapter of canons elect its president.

The Response: Negative.[106]

The issue here is whether the diocesan bishop can freely confer on a priest the presidency of a chapter of canons or whether one must be elected to that office.

Canon 157 states the general rule that "Unless otherwise explicitly determined by law, it is within the competence of the diocesan bishop to provide for ecclesiastical offices in his own particular church by free conferral." The question then is whether canon 509, §1, which deals specifically with the conferral of a canonry, explicitly determines that free conferral of the presidency of a chapter by the diocesan bishop is *not* permitted but rather that the president of a chapter must be elected. Canon 509, §1 reads as follows:

It is for the diocesan bishop, having listened to the chapter, but not for the diocesan administrator, to confer each and every individual canonry whether in the cathedral church or in the collegial church, every contrary privilege being revoked; it is for the same bishop to confirm the election by the chapter of the one who shall preside over it.

At first glance it might seem that the first part of this paragraph ("It is for the diocesan bishop . . .") deals with the *ordinary canonry*, while the second part of the paragraph ("It is for the same bishop . . .") deals with the *presidency*. Read in this way, the paragraph seems to be saying that the bishop can *appoint* a canon but that the president of the chapter must be *elected*, with the bishop confirming the election.

This reading of the 1983 law might seem, at least at a certain level, to tie in nicely with the 1917 law which definitely recognized a distinction in terms of conferral between an ordinary canonry and the presidency (or, for that matter, any "dignity"). In fact, however, the 1917 law on this point was quite different from that of the 1983 Code. The 1917 Code allowed, in canon 403, that a bishop could appoint a priest to an ordinary canonry but noted, in

[106]*AAS* 81 (1989) 991; *Periodica* 80 (1991) 127-130.

canon 396, §1, that the conferral of the presidency or of any other dignity was reserved to the Holy See.

By the time of the Second Vatican Council, however, the reservation of dignities to the Holy See was seen as an undue restriction on the diocesan bishop in the pastoring of his church, and *Christus Dominus* 28 said:

> In order to distribute the sacred ministries more equitably and properly among his priests, the bishop should possess a necessary freedom in assigning offices and benefices. Therefore, rights or privileges which in any way limit this freedom are to be suppressed.

Ecclesiae sanctae, the 1966 *motu proprio* on the implementation of certain Vatican II decrees, then went on to spell it out more explicitly. Norm 18. §1 said:

> The good of souls demands that the Bishop have proper freedom in conferring offices and benefices, even those to which the care of souls is not attached, fittingly and fairly upon the clerics who are best suited for them. The Apostolic See no longer reserves to itself the conferring of offices and benefices, whether connected with the care of souls or not, unless they are consistorial.[107]

In effect, therefore, the Second Vatican Council abolished any distinction between an ordinary canonry and the presidency insofar as their conferral is concerned. This was reflected in canon 157 of the 1983 Code which, as we have seen, provided that unless otherwise explicitly determined by law, a diocesan bishop could freely confer any ecclesiastical office in his own particular church.

When, therefore, canon 509, §1 is read in light of *Christus Dominus* 28, *Ecclesiae sanctae* 18. §1 and canon 157, it is clear that a diocesan bishop is free, in general, to appoint a priest to the presidency of a chapter of canons but that, if the statutes of a given chapter (which have, in accord with canon 505, been approved by the diocesan bishop) provide for the president to be elected, then it is for the diocesan bishop to confirm that election.

This response of the Commission is a SIMPLE DECLARATIVE one.

---

[107]*AAS* 58 (1966) 757; *CLD* 6: 275.

22. The Inability of the Diocesan Bishop to Tax the External Schools of Religious Institutes of Pontifical Right

The Doubt: Whether external schools of religious institutes of pontifical right are included under the words of canon 1263, "public juridic persons subject to his authority."

The Response: Negative.[108]

Canon 1263, one of the better known canons in the Code, deals with the taxing authority of the diocesan bishop. The opening words of this canon (which is the section that pertains to this response by the Commission) are: "The diocesan bishop has the right to impose a moderate tax on public juridic persons subject to his authority."

The question posed to the Commission has to do with the meaning or application of the phrase "public juridic persons subject to his authority." The Latin is *personis iuridicis publicis suo regimini subiectis.*[109] The Latin word *regimini*, which both the CLSA and the CLSGBI versions translate as "authority" in this context, can also be translated as "governance" or even "jurisdiction," as in canon 129, §1. The specific question before the Commission, then, is whether external schools[110] of religious institutes of pontifical right are or are not subject to the authority, governance or jurisdiction of the diocesan bishop.

Perhaps it should be noted, first of all, that most schools of religious institutes are not, in fact, established as public juridic persons in their own right but are rather *apostolates* of the public juridic person which is the institute. Since, however, canon 1263 permits the diocesan bishop to impose this ordinary tax only on public juridic persons, most schools of religious institutes are, in practice, exempt from this tax anyway, simply because they are not public juridic persons.

That having been said, however, what about external schools of religious institutes of pontifical right: are they or are they not subject to the authority of the diocesan bishop? It goes without saying, of course, that the institutes

---

[108]*AAS* 81 (1989) 991; *Periodica* 80 (1991) 108-127.

[109]Emphasis mine.

[110]That is to say ordinary Catholic schools open to all the faithful - as opposed to "internal" schools which are reserved for the training of candidates for religious life in a particular institute.

of pontifical right themselves are, by reason of canon 593, exclusively subject to the authority of the Holy See and are *not* subject to the authority of the diocesan bishop.[111] But what of the schools sponsored by those institutes?

Clearly external schools (but not internal schools) are subject to *visitation* by the diocesan bishop. Both *Ecclesiae sanctae* 39. 2[112] and canon 683, §1 state this explicitly. Thus canon 683 §1, says ". . . the diocesan bishop . . . can make a visitation of . . . schools . . . entrusted to religious; however he may not visit schools which are open only to students belonging to the institute."

It is equally clear that such schools are subject not just to visitation by the diocesan bishop but to his *vigilance* as well. Canon 806, §1 reads:

> The diocesan bishop has the right of vigilance over and visitation of the Catholic schools located in his territory, even those schools which have been established or are being directed by members of religious institutes; he is likewise competent to issue prescriptions dealing with the general regulation of Catholic schools; such prescriptions are also operative for those schools which are directed by religious, with due regard for their autonomy regarding the internal management of their schools.

To be subject to one's visitation and vigilance, however, is not necessarily to be subject to one's governance. Indeed, the final phrase of canon 806, §1 ("with due regard for their autonomy regarding the internal management[113] of their schools") makes it clear that while the diocesan bishop, in his role as chief pastor in the diocese, has the right to oversee religious education in the diocese, nevertheless religious institutes, at least those of pontifical right,[114] enjoy autonomy in the general governance of their schools.[115] The schools of religious institutes of pontifical right, therefore, are subject to the governance of the institute itself and not to the governance of the diocesan bishop. The Commission's response is a SIMPLE DECLARATIVE one.

[111]See also canons 312, 315 and 586.

[112]*AAS* 58 (1966) 773; *CLD* 6: 282.

[113]Both CLSA and the CLSGBI versions translate the Latin word *moderamen* as "management." It can, however, also be translated as "governance." See also *Ecclesiae sanctae* 39. §1 which uses the same word in recognizing the right of religious institutes to govern their own schools. *AAS* 58 (1966) 773; *CLD* 6: 282.

[114]And probably those of diocesan right as well, or so it would seem from the wording of canon 806, §1.

[115]The threefold distinction between visitation, vigilance and governance is also seen, though in a different context, in canon 305, §1.

58

23. The Sufficiency of a Relative Majority on the Third Ballot of an Election in accord with Canon 119, 1°

The Doubt: Whether, during elections held according to the norm of canon 119, 1° an absolute majority of votes of those present is required even on the third ballot, or whether, except in the case of a tie, a relative majority suffices.

The Response: Negative to the first part; affirmative to the second.[116]

Canon 119, 1°, which deals with elections, reads as follows:

If it is a question of elections, that action has the force of law which, when a majority of those who must be convoked are present, receives the approval of an absolute majority of those who are present; after two indecisive ballots, the choice is between the two candidates who have obtained the greater number of the votes, or, if there are several (with the same numbers), upon the two who are senior in age; after a third ballot, if the tie remains, the one who is the senior in age is considered elected.

Canon 119, 1° differs in many ways from its parallel canon in the 1917 Code, canon 101, §1, 1°, but in terms of this response by the Law Council,[117] the most *notable* difference is that the old canon 101, §1, 1° stated explicitly that a *relative* majority was sufficient on the third ballot whereas that phrase has not been retained in the present canon 119, 1°. The omission of the phrase, which must certainly have been intentional, has led some to wonder whether, for an election, an absolute majority is now required, even on the third ballot.

An absolute majority, incidentally, means more than half the votes, whereas a relative majority means more votes than those received by any other candidate.

Despite the solid foundation for the doubt, however, the response of the Law Council is both logical and practical. First of all, it is important to note

---

[116]*AAS* 82 (1990) 845; *Periodica* 80 (1991) 130-142.

[117]*Pastor bonus*, by which the name of the Code Commission was officially changed to "The Pontifical Council for the Interpretation of the Texts of Laws" (or "of Legislative Texts") took effect on March 1, 1989. This response, which was decided in a plenary meeting of May 8, 1990, was the first response of the dicastery under its new title. The previous response, n. 22, though published after March 1, 1989, had been decided before that date.

that both the former and new Codes make it quite clear that the maximum number of ballots allowed is three. After three ballots, according to our law, the matter must, in some way, be settled.

Imagine, then, the following, not untypical, scenario. A diocesan bishop dies. The diocesan consultors in that diocese number twelve, the maximum number allowed by canon 502, §1. In accord with canons 421, §1 and 176, all twelve consultors meet and elect the diocesan administrator as follows. On the first ballot, four priests: Matthew, the 55 year old fiscal officer; Mark, the 50 year old chancellor; Luke the 45 year old auxiliary bishop; and John, a 40 year old pastor, receive three votes each.

Since in this scenario of twelve consultors, an absolute majority would be seven, it is obvious that no one candidate is even close to an absolute majority. A discussion then follows during which it is made clear that, should the second ballot be a repeat of the first, then according to canon 119, 1°, Luke and John, as the two candidates junior in age, would be automatically eliminated from the third ballot. Nevertheless, on the second ballot, Matthew, Mark, Luke and John again receive three votes each.

On the third ballot it is between Matthew and Mark. There are now two basic possibilities. The first possibility is that all twelve consultors vote either for Matthew or Mark. This can result in one candidate receiving more votes than the other and thus winning by an absolute majority, i.e., by at least a seven to five vote; or it could result in a six to six tie, in which case Matthew, as the senior in age, is considered elected but by less than the seven votes needed for an absolute majority.[118] The second possibility is that one or more of the consultors who had originally backed either Luke or John are now reluctant to vote for either Matthew or Mark, and so they abstain. Even if there were only three abstentions, and therefore only nine effective votes, then the most likely result is that one of the candidates will win by either a five to four or a six to three vote (with the other candidate retaining the three votes he enjoyed from the beginning). So in this case we truly have a candidate elected by only a relative majority.

Since a scenario of this sort is not at all untypical, and since it may be presumed that the drafters of this canon had such scenarios in mind, it seems

---

[118]It would, of course, be incorrect to speak of Matthew being elected by a relative majority because, since it is a tie, it is, by definition not a majority at all. This explains the inclusion in the Doubt of the phrase "except in the case of a tie." Matthew is not actually elected but is considered elected by the law, so as to avoid a fourth ballot.

clear that this response of the Law Council is not an explanatory one. Since, however, canon 119, 1° does not in itself clearly allow a relative majority on the third ballot, especially when canon 119, 1° is read in light of the old canon 101, §1, 1°, the response should be considered QUASI-EXTENSIVE.[119]

[119]It is interesting to note that this scenario would have been played out differently under the old Code. Under canon 101, §1, 1° of that Code, Matthew, Mark, Luke and John would all have been eligible as candidates for the third ballot. If, after that ballot, all were still tied with three votes each, Luke, the auxiliary bishop, as the "senior in order" would be considered elected. See Charles Augustine, op. cit. II, 27, and Matthaeus Conte a Coronata, op. cit. I, 171. Without going into any detail perhaps the following outline of the differences between the Codes on this point will be of some help:

Item	1917	1983
Need for "Quorum"	Not explicit	A majority of those who must be convoked
Measure of Majority	Of those who voted (validly)	Of those present
Invalid Votes	Not to be counted	Irrelevant
Third ballot candidates	Indefinite number	Only two
Third ballot majority	Relative	Not mentioned
Presidential tie breaker	President may break	President may not break
Nonpresidential tie breaker	Senior by order	Senior in age

24. The Possibility of Bishops Emeriti Being Elected by Their Conference as Members of the Synod of Bishops

The Doubt: Whether bishops emeriti, as mentioned in canon 402, §1, can be elected by the conference of bishops as members of synods of bishops according to the prescriptions of canon 346, §1.

The Response: Affirmative.[120]

Christus Dominus 38, 2, Vatican II's Decree on the Bishops' Pastoral Office in the Church, notes the following regarding membership in a conference of bishops:

Members of the episcopal conferences are all local Ordinaries of every rite, coadjutors, auxiliaries, and other titular bishops who perform a special work entrusted to them by the Apostolic See or the episcopal conferences. Vicars general are not members. *De jure* membership belongs neither to other titular bishops nor, in view of their particular assignment in the area, to legates of the Roman Pontiff.

Article II b of the 1972 statutes of the National Conference of Catholic Bishops of the United States applies this explicitly to retired bishops by noting that bishops emeriti,

. . .while not considered *de iure* members according to the norms of *Christus Dominus*, retain membership in the Conference. This shall include the right to speak on all issues. The right to vote, however, shall extend to all matters except those which by law are binding when approved by two-thirds of the membership (cf. Article XIV) and those involving the acceptance of financial obligations (cf. Article XV).[121]

The NCCB statutes, which were, of course, approved by the Holy See, then go on in Article V, to restrict eligibility for office in the Conference only to *de iure* members.[122] According to the NCCB statutes, therefore, it would seem that bishops emeritii cannot be elected by the Conference to any office, including that of representing the Conference at a synod of bishops.

---

[120]*AAS* 83 (1991) 1093; *Periodica* 81 (1992) 347-350.
[121]*CLD* 7: 294.
[122]*CLD* 7: 295.

62

Nevertheless there is nothing, either in *Apostolica sollicitudo*, the 1965 *motu proprio* by which Pope Paul VI established the Synod of Bishops,[123] or in the Order of the Celebration of the Synod of Bishops[124] or in the *Code of Canon Law*, that would restrict a conference of bishops from electing a bishop emeritus to membership in the synod.

Apostolica sollicitudo, Article V, speaks only of: "the bishops elected by each of the national episcopal conferences as provided in n. VIII." And Article VIII likewise speaks only of "the bishops who represent each of the national conferences," without suggesting in any way that bishops emeriti might be excluded.[125]

The 1969 *Ordo Synodi*, in Articles 5, §1, 1°, b and 6, §1 again speaks only of "bishops" without a restriction of any kind.[126]

Finally, canon 346, §1 of the *Code of Canon Law* begins:

The membership of a synod of bishops gathered in ordinary general session consists of the following: for the most part, bishops elected to represent their individual groups by the conferences of bishops in accord with the special law of the synod.

Since, furthermore, synods are called in order to pool the wisdom of the universal episcopate on particular topics, e.g., evangelization, catechetics, the role of the family, the sacrament of reconciliation, the laity, it makes excellent sense to allow a conference of bishops the freedom to elect as its representative to a particular synod a bishop emeritus who might happen to be the member of the conference (even though not a *de iure* member) who is most knowledgeable on the topic under discussion at that synod.[127] The response of the Council is a SIMPLE DECLARATIVE one.

---

[123]*AAS* 57 (1965) 775-780; *CLD* 6: 388-393.

[124]The first *Ordo synodi* was published in 1966 (*AAS* 59 (1967) 91-103; *CLD* 6: 400-411). This was revised in 1969 (*AAS* 61 (1969) 525-539; *CLD* 7: 322-337). And there was a further emendation in 1971 (*AAS* 63 (1971) 702-704; *CLD* 7: 338-341).

[125]*CLD* 6: 390-391.

[126]*CLD* 7: 325-326.

[127]Indeed, on October 31, 1988, some three years before this response, the Congregation for Bishops issued *Norms concerning Bishops Ceasing from Office* in which, under n. 3, it specifically recommended that conferences of bishops consider electing to a synod of bishops those bishops emeriti "who are endowed with special competence and experience." *Communicationes* XX (1988) 168.

D. CONCLUDING OBSERVATIONS

1. The classifications assigned to each of the twenty-four responses are, of course, only my own personal opinion. Other canonists, better informed than I and of keener mind, might analyze and thus classify many of the responses differently.

The classifications as given, however, may be summarized schematically as follows. In order to save space I have used simple abbreviations (SD for Simple Declarative, QE for Quasi-Extensive etc.) for the eight categories:

SD	14	(2, 3, 5, 7, 8, 10, 11, 12, 14, 16, 19, 21, 22, 24)		
QE	2	(4, 23)	18	Declarative
QR	2	(6, 20)		

SE	1	(13)		
E	1	(18)	3	Explanatory
R	1	(1)		

UE	0	(though Navarrete considers 11 to be such)	3	Ultra-Explanatory
UR	3	(9, 15, 17)		

2. Gommar Michiels, in commenting on the authentic interpretation of law, made three rather general observations that bear repeating here: a) objectively doubtful laws are quite rare (*rariores*); b) authentic interpretations by the Code Commission are presumably declarative rather than explanatory; and c) the ultimate and decisive criterion which determines whether a law may be considered objectively doubtful is not the probable opinion of authors but the authentic judgment of the competent authority.[128]

3. Allow me to make a few comments applying Michiels' observations to the twenty-four responses as here classified:

---

[128]Gommarus Michiels, *Normae Generales Iuris Canonici* (Roma: Desclée, 1949) 490.

a. *The rarity of objectively doubtful laws.* Between January 1984, when the Code Commission was established, and January 1988, when Cardinal Castillo Lara gave his address to the Canon Law Society of Austria, more than 400 questions had been submitted to the Commission; of these, 32 were submitted to plenary examination; and of those 32, 15 had been published as authentic responses.[129]

Since that time, nine more responses have been published and it might be assumed that perhaps another 200 questions or so have been received by the Commission. It seems likely, in other words, that at least 600 questions have been submitted to the Commission/Council since January 1984.

It is, of course, precisely here, in this pool of some 600 or more questions, that any objectively doubtful laws that might exist in the new Code are likely to surface. According to my own examination of the twenty-four responses published to date, only six laws have been found to involve more than subjective doubt (as found in the three explanatory and three ultra-explanatory interpretations). This is a total of six out of perhaps 600 or more questions.

To say that something is "rare" or "quite rare" is, of course, to use a subjective form of measurement. What is rare to one person might not be to another; and what is rare in one situation might not be in another. Nevertheless when, after nine or ten years of fairly intense scrutiny by canonical scholars from all over the world, the meanings of only six laws have been found to involve more than subjective doubt, those six laws may, it seems, be safely described as "rare."

b. *The presumptive declarativeness of interpretations.* The principle that an authentic interpretation, especially of a canon in the Code, is presumably declarative rather than explanatory, is a sensible one. Each canon of the Code was, after all, drafted and redrafted, studied and restudied over a period of many years. Advice was sought from far and wide, and taken seriously. Each canon, in other words, was exquisitely crafted before being promulgated, so one is perfectly justified in presuming that once a canon is promulgated its meaning is intrinsically certain. Should, therefore, a doubt arise about the meaning of a particular canon, that doubt is presumably only a subjective doubt, and an authentic interpretation of that law is presumably only a declarative one.[130]

---

[129]*Communicationes* XX (1988) 276.
[130]See A4 above.

Anyone engaged in the examination and classification of authentic interpretations would be well advised to keep this principle in mind. At the same time, however, one must also keep in mind the principle that "a presumption cedes to the truth." Always, therefore, the search must be for the *truth*, which is usually but not always coterminous with the *presumed truth*. While it would, on the one hand, be rash to dismiss a recognized presumption as devoid of all wisdom, it would, on the other hand, be irresponsible and unscholarly to accept every presumption as the final word, and to allow that presumption to cut off all further inquiry.

The sensible approach, it would seem, to the classification of authentic interpretations, is to presume initially that a given interpretation is declarative, but then to examine the matter thoroughly. When the results of that examination dictate that, in fact, or in truth, this particular interpretation is not declarative but rather explanatory (or even ultra-explanatory) the usual presumption must then be at least tentatively set aside in favor of the truth as best the examiner understands it.

c. *The competent authority as final arbiter.* In theory there is no question but that the Code Commission/Law Council is the ultimate judge of whether a given interpretation is declarative or explanatory. In practice, however, the fact is that the Commission has almost never offered any specific directive on how a particular response is to be classified. We saw under B 2 that, in 1931, the Commission ruled that an earlier response declaring, despite the opposite opinion of most authors, that the phrase "born of non-Catholics" in canon 1099 §2 includes those born of parents only *one* of whom was non-Catholic, was a declarative and not an extensive one. But this was an extremely rare instance of a foray by the Commission into the realm of authentically classifying its own interpretations.

There was also the commentary issued by the President of the Law Council on Response Number 20 about the impossibility of an auxiliary bishop being elected to the presidency of a conference of bishops. At the conclusion of that commentary the Cardinal President noted that the Commission itself simply *issued* the response and did not deem it necessary to get into the business of *classifying* it, since such distinctions are, as he put it, usually left to "doctrine." The Cardinal did, however, suggest that most authors would probably see that interpretation as a declarative one.[131]

An unofficial commentary by the President of the Council, however, is, like the 1931 response mentioned above, extremely rare. Cardinal Castillo Lara probably saw this commentary on the relationship between an auxiliary bishop and the conference of bishops as a kind of experiment. If so, most canonists, I would think, would consider it to have been a highly successful one, and one which the President should perhaps utilize more often, especially in the more complex and subtle cases. Among the twenty-four responses given thus far, for example, a commentary by the President might have been particularly helpful regarding responses 9, 15 and 17, all of which I have reluctantly and tentatively classified as ultra-explanatory.

At any rate, while it is true in theory that the Commission/Council is the ultimate judge of such matters, in practice this dicastery tends to leave classification to the authors. There is always, of course, the general presumption that every authentic interpretation is declarative, and there is an even stronger presumption that, unless approved by the Pope with "specific approbation," no authentic interpretation is ultra-explanatory.[132] Beyond that, however, specific directives regarding classification are uncommon.

There is an old story about three baseball umpires who were asked how they distinguished balls from strikes. The first umpire said "Well, there are balls and there are strikes, and I calls 'em as I sees 'em." The second umpire said "There are balls and there are strikes, and I calls 'em as they is." And the third said "There are balls and there are strikes but they ain't nothin' till I calls 'em."

---

[131]*Communicationes* XXI (1989) 98. This Response number 20 was issued *before* March 1, 1989 (when the Commission became a Council), whereas the Cardinal's commentary on it was issued after that date.

[132]The second paragraph of Article 18 of the Apostolic Constitution *Pastor bonus* reads as follows: "Dicasteries are not able to pass laws or general decrees having the force of law nor are they able to derogate from prescripts of extant universal law except in individual cases and with the specific approbation of the Supreme Pontiff." *Communicationes* XX (1988) 22. For more on the meaning of the phrase "specific approbation" see Francisco J. Urrutia, "Quandonam Habeatur Approbatio 'In Forma Specifica'," *Periodica* 80 (1991) 3-17.

In his Vienna talk, Cardinal Castillo Lara made it clear that, as of that time (which included the first fifteen responses), no "specific approbation" had been issued. *Communicationes* XX (1988) 281.

Nor was there any mention of such approbation in the promulgation of response n. 17. AAS 80 (1988) 1818.

The mandate of the Code Commission/Law Council, as I understand it, is "to call 'em as they is," that is to say, to declare the true sense of the law. In general, the Commission/Council has admirably carried out that mandate. There have, however, been a few occasions, it seems, when the Commission has issued an interpretation that "wasn't nothin till it called it." It seems, in other words, that a few interpretations over the years have amounted to a materially new law that was nonexistent prior to the response by the Commission.

For my part, however, I just "calls 'em as I sees 'em," *salvo semper meliore iudicio Sanctae Sedis*.